C000090436

TROTT'S
PORCINE MISCELLANY

TROTT'S
PORCINE MISCELLANY

Conceived by

TROTT THE PIG

Written by Mike Darton

Ivy Press

First published in 2010 by
Ivy Press
210 High Street
Lewes
East Sussex BN7 2NS
United Kingdom
www.ivypress.co.uk

British Library Cataloguing-in-Publication Data
A catalogue record for this book is available from the British Library.

ISBN: 978-1-907332-29-6

Ivy Press
This book was conceived,
designed and produced by Ivy Press

Creative Director *Peter Bridgewater*
Publisher *Jason Hook*
Art Director *Wayne Blades*
Senior Editor *Polita Anderson*
Designer *Richard Constable*
Picture Research *Katie Greenwood*
Illustrations *Ivan Hissey*

Picture Acknowledgements
Bridgeman Art Library/Private Collection/Archives Charmet: 5
DK Images/Will Giles: 73.

Printed in India

1 3 5 7 9 10 8 6 4 2

*"I like pigs. A cat looks down on man,
a dog looks up to man — but a pig will look man
straight in the eye and see his equal."*

WINSTON CHURCHILL

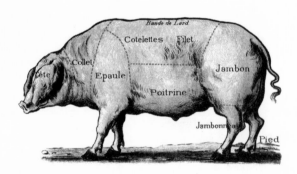

—————— THE PIG AS AN EVOLVED MAMMAL ——————

According to fossil evidence, pigs evolved during the Eocene epoch when the Artiodactyla (the even-toed ungulates) became differentiated from the Cetacea (which have since become the larger marine mammals), having in the previous Palaeocene epoch had a common ancestry (the Cetartiodactyla).

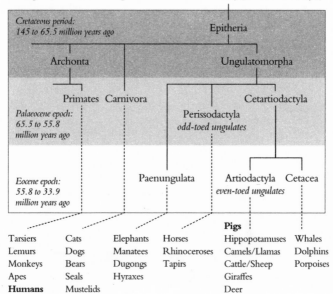

Cretaceous period: 145 to 65.5 million years ago	Epitheria				
Archonta		Ungulatomorpha			
Primates Carnivora			Cetartiodactyla		
Palaeocene epoch: 65.5 to 55.8 million years ago		Perissodactyla *odd-toed ungulates*			
Eocene epoch: 55.8 to 33.9 million years ago	Paenungulata		Artiodactyla *even-toed ungulates*	Cetacea	

				Pigs	
Tarsiers	Cats	Elephants	Horses	Hippopotamuses	Whales
Lemurs	Dogs	Manatees	Rhinoceroses	Camels/Llamas	Dolphins
Monkeys	Bears	Dugongs	Tapirs	Cattle/Sheep	Porpoises
Apes	Seals	Hyraxes		Giraffes	
Humans	Mustelids			Deer	

THE EVOLUTION of all the mammal species – of which this chart shows a selection from perhaps only about 60% – has become subject to some dispute since the 1990s, following genetic research involving DNA comparison. The areas of dispute relate not only to the historical time at which individual species may first have appeared but even to some of the formerly accepted links between certain orders and families.

It must also be remembered that the domestic pig (which is what most people now think of generally as the classic pig) is not a product of genuine evolution at all but an animal that humans brought into being by domestication and selective breeding among wild boars from about 10,000 years ago – which in evolutionary terms is a very short time. The domestic pig has since come to vastly outnumber its wilder relatives, some of which are in real danger of following earlier relatives to extinction.

In 2009, authorities variously calculated that at that time there were somewhere between 850 million and 2 billion live domestic pigs.

RISE & SWINE

A selection of pig alarm clocks is available from a number of online shopping sites. Most of them feature an image of a pig's face on the dial, and almost all of them use the sound of one or more pigs as the actual alarm, often described in the accompanying literature as "oinking you awake". Some websites advertise the clocks as arousing a sleeper to the "reassuringly rural" sounds of the farmyard … but it must be wondered how many households would welcome such a clock as a gift, given the implication that, even without the clock, farmyard sounds were ordinarily to be heard in the bedroom first thing in the morning.

THE PORCINE PALATE

THE PIG'S tongue has around 19,800 taste buds (humans have around 10,600). This means that the pig can taste about 50% *more* than humans with the tastebuds on the back of the tongue, and as much as 200% *more* than humans with the tastebuds on the tip of the tongue. Despite this, no provision for the pig's sense of taste has ever been made in any of the major textbooks on pig diet and nutrition, not even in relation to the synthesis of a number of new sweetening substances available since the 1970s – although pigs are well documented as having a sweet tooth. It is known that pigs drink up to six times their usual daily amount of water if a small proportion of sucrose is added.

At the same time, pigs' better sense of taste might make them more discriminatory than humans about what is sweet to them and what is not. In the 1990s an experiment was undertaken to test an array of 13 substances that were sweet to humans on a group of pigs. The pigs found only three of them to be what *they* thought of as genuinely sweet.

HOGGING THE SHOW

There are six major traits which judges at a pig show look for:

❋ *soundness* – that is, correct growth and even development, particularly of the legs, enabling smooth walking and a comfortable gait
❋ *good muscling* – that is, muscles across the body, particularly the hams, that are long and smooth, not short and bunched
❋ *freedom from excess fat* – the ideal pig is a lean pig
❋ *a wide body* – again indicating correct growth and firm muscling
❋ *a longish frame size* – that is, a skeletal frame that displays a relatively long neck, long body and long legs
❋ *"eye appeal"* – that is, a proportionately pleasing overall appearance with no evident defects.

ST PAUL, MINNESOTA

Sᴛ Pᴀᴜʟ ɪs ᴛʜᴇ ᴄᴀᴘɪᴛᴀʟ and second most populous city of the ᴜs state of Minnesota. But the original name of the settlement was Pig's Eye, so called – according to the city's tourist literature and website – after the French-Canadian whiskey trader Pierre "Pig's Eye" Parrant, who had led squatters to the settlement. This description, however, somewhat euphemistically glosses over the fact that Pig's Eye Parrant was an ex-fur-trapper who, blinded in one eye, became a moonshine bootlegger. He set up a hard-liquor bar which he called Pig's Eye Pandemonium in what was then a secluded area, and which thereafter drew all the labouring men of the vicinity to it like a magnet, some of whom set up a more or less permanent camp around it. Over time the little community became a village, with a high street and stores, and eventually even a church. In fact, it was the Catholic priest – one Lucien Galtier – sent to the church there who was so appalled by the name Pig's Eye and its bluntly profane derivation that he decided it should be converted from ungodliness to saintliness, just as St Paul had been in the New Testament. And he renamed the place St Paul accordingly.

PIG LATIN

One of the great jokes in the equivalent of schoolrooms in ancient Rome – and repeated as a matter of ponderously erudite humour by classics masters in

many English public schools – was the Latin sentence: *Mea mater est mala sus*, which can mean either of two things: "My mother is an evil pig", or "Get a move on, mother – the pig is scoffing the apples."

THE PORCINARIUM

Pʀᴏʙᴀʙʟʏ ᴛʜᴇ ᴡᴏʀʟᴅ's ᴏɴʟʏ museum devoted entirely to real and historic pigs, the Porcinarium, is part of the Animal Improvement Institute of the Agriculture Research Council, situated just outside the small township of Irene, south of Pretoria, in South Africa. Displayed with the help of the Transvaal Museum, the exhibits are intended mainly to show the origin and development of pig species in southern Africa. The museum's official opening coincided with the 40th anniversary of the South African National Pig Performance Testing Scheme in August 1996. It is open to the public during office hours on weekdays, and by private appointment during weekends otherwise.

——————————————— PIG BREEDS ———————————————

There are generally acknowledged to be 73 different pig breeds, some of which have been associated for much longer with their locations – and are therefore regarded as more traditional – than others. They are:

American landrace......	German landrace.......	Mukota..............
American Yorkshire	Gloucestershire old spot..	Mulefoot ....
Angeln saddleback......	Guinea hog..........	
Arapawa Island		Neijiang ....
	Hampshire	Ningxiang............
Ba Xuyen	Hereford.............	Norwegian landrace ....
Bantu	Hezuo	
Bazna		Ossabaw Island ....
Beijing black..........	Iberian	Oxford sandy and black ..
Belarus black pied	Italian landrace	
Belgian landrace		Philippine native ....
Bentheim black pied	Jinhua..............	Pietrain..............
Berkshire		Poland China ....
Black Slavonian........	Kele	
British landrace	Krskopolje	Red wattle ....
British lop............	Kune kune	
Bulgarian white........		Saddleback ....
	Lacombe.............	Spots................
Cantonese............	Large black	Swabian-Hall ....
Chester white	Large black-and-white...	Swedish landrace.......
Czech improved white ..	Large white..........	
	Lithuanian native.......	Tamworth ....
Danish landrace........		Thuoc Nhieu ....
Dermantsi pied	Mangalitsa...........	Tibetan..............
Duroc...............	Meishan	Turopolje ....
Dutch landrace	Middle white	
	Minzhu..............	Vietnamese potbellied ...
Fengjing	Mong Cai............	
Finnish landrace	Mora Romagnola	Welsh...............
French landrace........	Moura	Wuzhishan ....

A fair number of these are landrace pigs. "Landrace" is originally a Danish term, which means precisely "race (of pig that lives in/on the) land" – that is, the standard type of pig familiar in the countries of mostly northern Europe – and specifically the type from which the world-famous Danish bacon is produced. "Pied" describes pigs that in pig-breeders' terms are "black and white", although black may be anything from dark grey to navy blue, and white may be anything from yellowish through light pink to light grey. A saddleback has a lighter- or darker-coloured hoop of indeterminate size around the mid-body.

PIG IN A CHINA SHOP

Porcelain is a type of high-quality ceramic with a glassily translucent surface. Its English name is derived originally from Italian *porcellana*, the word for a certain kind of seashell which has a very shiny surface, and which was so called because in shape the shell resembles the back or underpart of a female piglet (Italian *porcella*). In one form or another the word *porcelain* is to be found in most European languages, although more disguised in some than others (for example, German *Porzellan*, Croatian *porculan*, Welsh *porslen*, Swedish *porslin* and Finnish *posliini*).

THE FACTS OF LIFE FOR A FARM PIG

SOME FOUR MONTHS – actually, by long-standing rural tradition, "three months, three weeks and three days" – after successful (and usually artificial) insemination, a sow gives birth to between six and 22 piglets. Ten is the most common number, of which on average 8.5 survive. The piglets drink their mother's milk (as "sucklings") for about five weeks, and then begin to eat solid food (as "weanlings").

Pigs of both sexes generally become sexually competent at around the age of eight months, although a female's first oestrus (regular sexual preparedness) may be delayed by any of various factors for up to ten months more. Most farm sows spend at least two-thirds of their entire lives thereafter in pregnancy.

Other than for the large proportion of pigs sent to slaughter at between four and seven months of age, the average lifespan of a farm pig is between four and five years (whereas a natural lifespan has been calculated as between 10 and 15 years).

AESOP'S FABLE OF THE LION & THE BOAR

It was a hot summer day in a dry and dusty region of Africa. The animals at a remote water-hole scattered regretfully when they saw a lion and a boar approaching from different directions. Both reached the abruptly deserted water's edge at the same moment. Neither would let the other drink before him, and a bloody battle for supremacy ensued. It went on and on, though both lion and boar quickly became tired and sore from the wounds they sustained. Finally, by unspoken agreement, they sat back and panted for a while. And as they did, they spotted the vultures circling patiently overhead, waiting to dine on the eventual loser.

The battle was at once forgotten, for in the minds of both lion and boar it seemed infinitely preferable to stay alive and drink together as friends than to die and become food for vultures.

BIBLICAL PIGS

Pigs are mentioned in the Judaeo-Christian Bible (the Old Testament) six times – twice to the effect that they are "unclean" animals, three times to the effect that human consumption of any part of a pig corresponds to "an abomination", and once in the form of this simile:

> *'As a jewel of gold in a swine's snout,*
> *so is a fair woman which is without discretion.'*
> PROVERBS 11:22

In the (Christian) New Testament, pigs are mentioned no fewer than 13 times, although 10 of them are references to the herd of Gadarene swine (pigs from an area east of the Sea of Galilee) into which Jesus cast devils or unclean spirits. Two other references are in the story of the Prodigal Son, who at one desperate stage wanted to eat the husks he had been given to feed the pigs, before he realised the error of his ways and returned penitently to his supernaturally patient father. And the final reference relates to the well-known admonition not to "cast pearls before swine".

WHAT PIGS SEE

Pigs rely on smelling and hearing more than they do on seeing. This is at least partly because their eyes are so far apart as to be on each side of the head rather than both at the front. There is only a 35° to 50° overlap of forward vision, whereas each eye has around 140° of lateral vision.

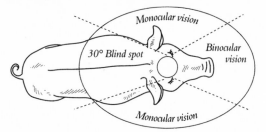

Pigs therefore tend to be far more visually aware of things either side of them than of things in front – which is important to remember when trying to get them to move in a direction you want them to go, especially within a confined space. Naturally perceived only in two dimensions, not three, any visual distraction on one side or the other – a change in floor surface, perhaps, or a difference in the balance of light – will cause a pig to stop dead, sniff and raise the ears in an attempt to use what to the pig are its more immediate means of obtaining sensory information.

—————————— BLACK PIG'S DYKE ——————————

BLACK PIG'S DYKE is a straggling series of ancient ditches connecting areas of bogland, which formed a boundary between the old rival provinces of Ulster and Connacht in Ireland in the first century AD. It is said that it was created when a huge wild boar destroyed the Viking stronghold at Armagh (which in fact existed some eight or nine centuries later) and proceeded to ravage the countryside with its tusks, first in a southwesterly direction, then turning northwest towards Donegal. Certainly the boar – which had no bristles and was therefore "black" – has been a figure of local superstition for more than a millennium, held to represent death and the embodiment of evil.

—————————— PERFORMING PIGS ——————————

Because they are so intelligent, pigs can be trained to perform quite a number of different activities on command. However, training often involves removing the pigs from their normal sedentary outdoor lifestyle, and this in turn can lead to psychological stress and consequent aggressive behaviour.

—————————— WHAT IS SWINE FLU? ——————————

SWINE FLU is an infection by any of the swine influenza viruses (SIVs) – types of influenza virus that are endemic in pigs – notably the influenza C virus and the strains of influenza A known scientifically as H1N1, H1N2, H3N1, H3N2 and H2N3. These viral disorders are very common in pigs all over the world and every year contribute to considerable economic losses in the pig-farming industry. Symptoms in infected pigs include high temperature, respiratory difficulties (with coughing and sneezing), reduced appetite and consequent weight loss. Fatalities are, however, rare.

It is also rare for humans to contract the virus. (It is actually slightly less unusual for pigs to catch flu from humans.) And when humans do become infected by an SIV – often only after prolonged and continuous proximity to infected pigs – noticeable symptoms may anyway be entirely absent, the only bodily effect being the production of antibodies in the bloodstream. At the same time, the contracting of *any* flu virus represents some risk to vulnerable people.

—————————— VAIN PURSUITS ——————————

'Men should worry about achieving glory just as pigs about being fat.'
CHINESE PROVERB

THE PIG AS MEAT

The major divisions of a pig carcase are shown below. Listed beneath are how the carcase is divided into cuts and joints of meat.

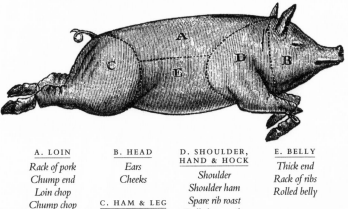

A. LOIN	B. HEAD	D. SHOULDER, HAND & HOCK	E. BELLY
Rack of pork	*Ears*	*Shoulder*	*Thick end*
Chump end	*Cheeks*	*Shoulder ham*	*Rack of ribs*
Loin chop		*Spare rib roast*	*Rolled belly*
Chump chop	**C. HAM & LEG**	*Rolled spare ribs*	
Escalope	*Rolled pork leg*	*Picnic ham*	
Tenderloin	*Ham*	*Trotter*	
	Pork leg		

The ears are considered a delicacy, particularly in Chinese, Japanese and Spanish cuisine, and also occasionally appear as a "soul food" ingredient eaten by African-Americans in the southern USA. Pigs' tails may be boiled in a stew or soup, or – rarely – served fried in similar areas of the world. Trotters (called crubeens in Ireland), however, are included in recipes worldwide, often to take advantage of their high gelatine content.

Bacon is thin slices of fatty meat cured primarily with salt or in brine, taken from the loin or from the sides of the belly. In the USA, bacon is almost always only from the belly, whereas in northwestern Europe "back bacon" is from the loin, and "streaky bacon" is from the belly sides. Some countries prefer bacon also to be smoked after curing. In central and southern Europe, unsmoked bacon is prepared in the form of lardons (small cubes) that can be added for flavour and extra fat to other cooked dishes.

Something that cannot be shown diagrammatically but that in many areas of the world is regarded as an important part of the "meat" derived from the pig is the blood. This is used primarily to produce blood sausage ("black pudding" in English, and dialectal names in many other languages, particularly Slavonic and Latin American) and blood pancakes, often with a cereal or rice basis.

———————— PEARLS BEFORE SWINE ————————

In the (Christian) New Testament of the Bible – Matthew 7:6 (part of the celebrated Sermon on the Mount) – Jesus is described as saying:

> Give not that which is holy unto the dogs, neither cast ye your pearls before swine, lest they trample them under their feet, and turn again and rend you.

This is always taken to mean that you should never give things of value to those who will not appreciate them and may even resent your offering, to the extent of doing you harm. It could equally mean, though, that you should not try to press your own religious faith on those who are already fully committed to another. It is interesting, however, that an apparent comparison is made between dogs and pigs – and the pigs are apparently the more dangerous.

———————— THE PIG AS ARTIODACTYL ————————

It was the appearance of the first grasses during the early Eocene epoch that enabled the Artiodactyla (the even-toed ungulates) to evolve further and faster than the hitherto more successful Perissodactyla (the ancestors of the horses and rhinoceroses). This is notably because their digestive systems adapted to take advantage of the abundance of the new food source even though it was of relatively low nutritional value. Four major suborders of artiodactyls emerged (or five, if you consider whales and hippopotamuses to be separate suborders).

✱ **The ruminants** – such as modern cows, sheep and goats, which have multiple stomachs.
✱ **The tylopods** – such as modern camels, llamas and vicunas, which rely on liquid intake and storage to eke out the food supply.
✱ **The cetancodonts** – currently regarded as comprising both hippopotamuses and the larger marine mammals, which conserve energy by swimming.
✱ **The pigs** – which have a fairly simple digestive system but (at least in the wild) still depend on low-growing vegetation – and lots of it.

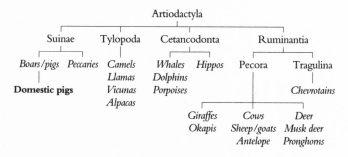

THE PATRON SAINT OF SWINEHERDS

The patron saint of swineherds is St Anthony the Great, better described as Antony of Egypt (251–356) who, although in some ways the inspiration for the earliest Christian enclosed monastic orders, had virtually nothing whatever to do with pigs. It was some 640 years after his death that the Order of Hospitallers of St Antony was founded at La Motte, in France, the main buildings of which became a centre of pilgrimage for the sick and suffering, some of whom were miraculously healed. Monks of this order roamed far and wide, ringing little bells to encourage alms-giving by local people. The order was permitted to let its pigs roam the streets with the monks by special dispensation. Thereafter, the emblems associated with Antony were bells and a pig.

SWEATING LIKE A PIG

In the second half of the 20th century, this used to be a fairly common expression in English after unaccustomed exertion. But pigs *don't* sweat. They do have some sweat glands in their skin but these can diffuse only a minimal  amount of liquid through the skin to dissipate heat. Instead, pigs rely on conductive cooling for thermoregulation – that is, lying on a colder surface, especially a surface that is sloppily moist (not actually wet) and thus unlikely to warm up too quickly to body temperature. Mud is excellent in this regard. And unlike sweating, this process does not involve a loss of body fluids that might result in dehydration. Moreover, the mud, when drying on the skin, acts as a sort of sunscreen to protect the pig from sunburn – to which pigs are particularly liable – and as a temporary defence against flies and other bothersome insects.

FEAR OF FLU

In Afghanistan (where pork and pig products are banned for religious reasons), there is only one pig known to be resident – kept in a cage together with goats and deer in the zoo in Kabul. In May 2009, news agency Reuters reported that it had been confined to a small room by itself 'under quarantine' because visitors to the zoo had complained they might catch swine flu from it. This was unfortunate for the wretched pig in view of the fact that transmission of the swine influenza virus (SIV) from pig to human occurs only by direct and continuous contact usually with more than one affected pig. Moreover, the inhabitants of Kabul were far more likely to contract the disease from other humans, notably those who had travelled to parts of Europe, North America, Central America, the Far East and/or Australia.

——————————— PIGS & ROBBERS ———————————

IT WAS IN THE MID-1960S that viewers of US TV police crime-and-detection series might have been (at least initially) shocked to hear the police being called not just "the cops" but "the pigs". "Pig", after all, is in quite a few languages (including French and German) a term of abuse, but this usage was perhaps more carefully casual than abusive, although it must still have been resented by the police officers of the time. Yet "pig" as a term for a law officer is far older than the 1960s. In fact, the earliest printed record of the term in that usage dates from 1811, apparently in London, England, in relation to a Bow Street Runner.

——————————— HOG'S BACK, THE WORLD OVER ———————————

✱ *The Hog's Back* – part of the North Downs, Surrey, southeastern England, between Farnham and Guildford
✱ *The Hog's Back Falls* (officially but rarely called the Prince of Wales Falls) – a cascade of artificial rapids on the Rideau River in Ottawa, Canada, just north of where the Rideau Canal splits off
✱ *Hogsback, Eastern Cape, South Africa* – a scenic tourist village and nature reserve near three prominent mountain ridges said to resemble bristles on a hog's back
✱ *The Hogsback* – a precipitous section of mountain road in southern Utah, USA, between Calf Creek and Boulder
✱ *Hogs Back* – promontory on the isle of Sark, Channel Islands, off northern France, reached by a narrow road causeway with precipitous cliff sides
✱ *Hogsback* – name of a steep climb on the south side of Mt Hood, Washington State, USA, not far from Mt St Helens and Mt Rainier
✱ *Hogs Back* – a virtual reality for *MechWarrior4: Vengeance* games.

——————————— A LITTLE PIG GOES A LONG WAY ———————————

THE MOVIE *Babe* – of which "A little pig goes a long way" is the subtitle – was made in 1995 primarily in Robertson, New South Wales, Australia, and features the story of a young pig that wishes to be a sheepdog. A combination of real and animatronic pigs and border collies, together with award-winning visual effects particularly for the dialogue, give a startlingly "realistic" presentation. The movie was released on video in 1996 and on DVD in 1999. By 2001 it was also possible to buy on DVD the 1998 movie sequel, *Babe: Pig in the City* (subtitle: "In the heart of the city, a pig with heart").

---------------------------- THE WHOLE HOG ----------------------------

The healthy pig is active and alert, and seems interested in life. It eats well and consistently, it has a sleek haircoat, and its tail is tightly curled. Its body temperature is 39.2°C (102.5°F). There are many signs that a pig is, conversely, feeling under the weather. Apart from not eating well, a rough haircoat and listlessness, there may be diarrhoea, coughing and/or an unwillingness to move. On the occurrence of any combination of these signs, the pig's temperature should be taken. If it is two degrees or more above normal, a vet should be called. Most common pig disorders and ailments can be successfully treated and cured – if the treatment begins early enough.

---------------------------- THE PIG FAMILY ----------------------------

THE PIG FAMILY (Suidae) is classically represented by the *Sus* genus to which the domestic pig belongs. However, it must be pointed out at once that the domestic pig is in fact a subspecies of the wild boar, *Sus scrofa*, and that there are other members of the *Sus* genus, which are species in their own right. The full list is thus like this:

Wild boar . . . . *Sus scrofa*	**Vietnam warty pig**. . . *Sus bucculentus*
Domestic pig . . . . *S. scrofa domestica*	**Visayan warty pig** . . . . . .*S. cebifrons*
	Mindoro warty pig . . . . . . *S. oliveri*
Bearded pig. . . . .*Sus barbatus*	**Philippine warty pig** . *S. philippensis*
Palawan bearded pig *S. ahoenobarbus*	**Java warty pig** . . . . *S. verrucosus*

Other members of the Suidae not taxonomically classified as belonging to the *Sus* genus include: from sub-Saharan Africa, the red river hog (*Potamochoerus porcus*) and bushpig (*P. larvatus*), the forest hog (*Hylochoerus meinertzhageni*) and the warthogs (*Phacochoerus* sp), and from Indonesia the enormous-tusked babirousa (*Babyrousa* sp). The Himalayan pygmy hog (formerly *Sus salvanius*) is now classified as *Porcula salvania*.

---------------------------- THE PIG & THE PIBROCH ----------------------------

'I understand the inventor of the bagpipes was inspired when he saw a man carrying an indignant, asthmatic pig under his arm. Unfortunately, the manmade sound never equalled the purity of the sound achieved by the pig.'
ALFRED HITCHCOCK (1899–1980), *Film director*

SPOILED PIGS ALL

"Give to a pig when it grunts and to a child when it cries, and you will have a fine pig and a bad child."

DANISH PROVERB

PIGS IN SPACE

In modern astronomical catalogues and charts there are no constellations at all named after any of the family Suidae – which makes it very unusual, for most mammalian groups are represented in the night sky in one form or another. The situation is similar with the names of individual stars, although that may not be too surprising because many star names derive from Arabic and the Arabs (like most Semitic peoples) regard the pig as an animal generally unworthy of special attention.

But away from Arabic influences, pigs were not always left out in the cold, astronomically speaking.

The two known exceptions of this kind are:

★ the star cluster called the Hyades (in the constellation Taurus), which rural folk in Italy during ancient Roman times called Suculae, "the piglets";

★ the constellation Orion, which seems to have been alternatively known by the Anglo-Saxons as "the boar-throng".

MICRO PIG PETS

MICRO PIGS ARE CROSS-BREEDS between miniature pot-bellied pigs and Tamworths, Kune Kunes and Gloucester Old Spots. They are tiny but perfectly-formed pigs that in two years from birth are fully grown yet only some 33 centimetres (13 inches) tall and a maximum of 29.5 kilograms (65 pounds, 4⅔ stone) in weight. Advertised as "fantastic pets ... low-maintenance ... easy to toilet-train ... very loving", they have since the mid-1980s become popular as house pets for the young well-to-do in North America and northern Europe.

But there are some severe drawbacks to having a micro pig as a house pet, as outlined by more than one expert on pig husbandry. Pigs are essentially outdoor animals and may become aggressive and destructive when kept indoors, biting their owners and wreaking havoc with furniture and curtains. Moreover, in most countries they are classified as herd farm animals and must be registered and licensed as such, which involves the continual keeping of records on medical health and any medical treatment the pig receives, on feeding regimes (with schedule and quantities) and on any changes of location.

BIG PIG

THE LARGEST PIG in recorded history would seem to have been "Bill", owned by Burford Butler of Jackson, Tennessee, USA. In 1933, Bill weighed a massive 1,157.59 kilograms (2,552 pounds or 1.16 tonnes), was 2.47 metres (9 feet) long, and even with his belly dragging along the ground – since he was physically unable to move otherwise – was 1.5 metres (5 feet) tall.

More recently, a pig reared in China was officially weighed at 898.1 kilograms (1,980 pounds) and was 2.51 metres (8 foot 3 inches) long with a circumferential girth of only just less. It was being groomed for stardom – Chinese statisticians (not to mention senior politicians) hoped to beat all records – when in 2007 the pig succumbed to heart failure through lack of exercise, and expired on the spot.

GRISEBRØNDEN

THE CITY OF AARHUS (Århus), Denmark, prides itself on being the cultural capital of Jutland, a shining example of the nation's heritage. At the foot of the tall building that is the City Hall, in the main City Square, is a fountain known as *Grisebrønden*, "the pigs' fountain", which features a multiplicity of jets of water spurting in many directions. The basic sculpture of the fountain is a contented, if somewhat unusually sharp-nosed, sow with a number of piglets in close attendance. The ensemble is brightly described in tourist literature as "drooling and peeing".

Enough said. It really is nothing like The Little Mermaid in Copenhagen.

GONE FERAL

Over the last 50 years, the accidental (or deliberate) release of domestic pigs into areas and environments where they constitute an alien species has caused considerable local disruption. The pigs' omnivorous diet, their aggressive behaviour in unfamiliar surroundings and the way they rootle with their snouts in and on the ground may overturn an intricately balanced ecosystem that has no residual defences. Pigs may eat small animals that do not see them coming, and may destroy the ground-level nests or scrapes of birds that are accustomed to quite different forms of predator. The Invasive Species Specialist Group, a commission run under the auspices of the International Union for the Conservation of Nature, includes feral pigs on the list of the world's 100 worst invasive species.

TRAINING YOUR PIG FOR A SHOW

Begin training your pig some weeks before a show, so that the pig knows something about what to expect to have to do, even if the environment is unfamiliar. Training predominantly involves getting your pig to move easily at a walk when and where you require. A cane with a curved end (handle) is recommended for urging and guiding the pig forward, tapping gently with the curved end behind the front flank or on the side. Never hit the pig on the back or the rump – and never, *never*, under any circumstances, touch the pig's snout.

THE GOLDEN-BRISTLED BOAR

In Norse mythology, Gullinbursti ("golden-bristled") was a boar magically forged in the furnace of the dwarf brothers Brokkr and Sindri (also known as Eitri) in response to a wager set by the god Loki that they could not fashion anything so marvellous as the three items Loki had purloined: a spear from the chief god Odin, a ship from the great goddess Freya and the golden hair of the giantess Sif. The forging took considerable time and effort, as detailed in the *Prose Edda*, but the finished creation was indeed marvellous.

What was so special about Gullinbursti was not just – as Brokkr boasted – that the boar could travel through air and water better than any horse, but that the bristles in its golden mane glowed with light that lit up the trees on the earth, the sky above and the sea below.

In one version of the story, Brokkr gave Gullinbursti to Freya's brother Frey, who used the boar as one of two that pulled his divine chariot. In another version, Freya herself received the boar and was able to travel on its back from her own Hall of half of the glorious slain to Odin's Hall of the other half of the glorious slain (Valhalla), using the light emanating from its mane to penetrate the darkness on the way.

ARE GUINEA PIGS PIGS?

No. They are neither pigs nor do they come from Guinea. And yet in many languages of the world (including German, Swedish, French, Italian and Russian) they are descriptively called little pigs.

In fact, they are rodents and they originate in the Andes mountain ranges of South America. Belonging to the genus *Cavia* (hence the English alternative name, cavey), the species is not like other members of the same genus, however, because they have been domesticated for so long – and have meanwhile been bred for certain useful properties – that they now no longer exist naturally in the wild. The most useful of those useful properties is of course that the guinea pig, just like a real pig, makes excellent eating.

────────────── VIIVI & WAGNER ──────────────

Viivi & Wagner is a serial comic strip involving two characters who might for all the world be just another married couple. They appear to cohabit relatively amicably, with a modicum of genial bickering, but they have many mutual interests, especially political events elsewhere in the world and the serious literature of other countries. The one difference between Viivi & Wagner and other couples is that although Viivi is a pleasant and very articulate woman in her twenties, Wagner is a mature male pig: an actual pig – who speaks equally articulately.

The comic strip, which is now famous throughout northern Europe but not well known in English-speaking countries, originated in a promotional magazine (*Kultapossu*, "Golden-piggy") for children issued by a bank in Finland, created and drawn by "Juba" Tuomola. Wagner in this way began as a talking piggy bank. When for one reason or another the magazine ceased production, Tuomola restructured his creation on an adult basis, in the process re-characterising his principals – and has not looked back since.

────────────── THE WARTY PIGS ──────────────

WARTY PIGS are to be found almost solely on the islands of Indonesia and the Philippines (other than in zoos across the world, often sponsored by the Philippine government conservation agency). They are called warty pigs because of the pairs of what people might consider unsightly growths on the sides and underneath their long-snouted faces and jowls. It is ordinarily only the males that visibly have these growths, and then only in advanced age, when the growths can make them appear alarmingly grotesque, especially alongside the smaller, more natural-looking females. In the wild – in their tropical forest habitat – warty pigs are mostly secretive and retiring, although when cornered they can be viciously dangerous. In Indonesia, the pigs sometimes undertake seasonal migrations linked apparently to the monsoon. However, the habitats of all the warty pigs are shrinking and disappearing through human encroachment, and most of them are now on the severely endangered list. It is thought that the Vietnam warty pig (*Sus bucculentus*) has recently become extinct for this same reason.

────────────── PORCUS SAPIENS ──────────────

"The creatures outside looked from pig to man, and from man to pig, and from pig to man again; but already it was impossible to say which was which."
GEORGE ORWELL (ERIC ARTHUR BLAIR, 1903–1950),
Animal Farm (1945), Chapter 10

—————————— PORK & APPLE SAUCE ——————————

To eat pork – particularly roast pork or grilled pork chops – with apple sauce seems to have been a northern European tradition since medieval times when servants carried in boars' heads on trays as the centrepiece of a banquet, and each boar's head had an apple in its mouth. Today's apple sauce is simply diced cooking apples boiled into a mush and puréed further, to which cinnamon, nutmeg or allspice may be added together with any of various sweeteners. This form of preparation tends to remove much of the cooking apples' original acidic tartness, which must surely have been the main reason for the medieval combination with the succulent and savoury roast meat.

—————————— OF SOWS' EARS & SILK PURSES ——————————

It was the Irish poet and cleric Jonathan Swift (1667–1745), author of the world-renowned *Gulliver's Travels* (1726), who popularised the English expression – by then already proverbial for around 150 years – that "you can't make a silk purse out of a sow's ear". It means that it is impossible to make something valuable out of something that is basically worthless to begin with. The expression has recently led to the invention of the phrase "the sow's ear effect" in international finances. This is what happens when a nation state is unable to increase its productivity or per capita GDP at the rate or to the level of other countries of similar political development, even by making adjustments to its macroeconomic policy (perhaps because its labour force is under-skilled).

—————————— BERTA, OPERA STAR ——————————

In May 2004 it was announced in the German musical press that a live pig would be required to appear on stage as an extra in the Krefeld-Moenchengladbach Theater's production of the opera *Martha* by Friedrich von Flotow (1812–1883). The first and last Acts of the opera include a market scene (the subtitle of the opera is actually *Richmond Market*), and the pig would be there as part of the background in the portrayal of an everyday English market during the mid-1840s. Six pigs were registered for an audition. Three of them failed to turn up – two because they showed signs of stress, and one because its transport got stuck in a traffic jam – and of the remaining three the pot-bellied Berta finally landed the role. Her main qualification was apparently the ability "just to stand about and simply be a pig", although the fact that she was the least stressed (and therefore presumably the most static and silent), as certified by the opera company's hired vet, probably helped. Regrettably, however, not a single media review of the eventual production is available that contains any reference whatsoever to Berta's performance.

TUSK MANAGEMENT

Pigs have a full set of 44 teeth. (Humans have a maximum of 32.) The canine teeth – the tusks – in boars grow continuously and are sharpened by other teeth on the upper and lower jaws which rub against each other. Farmers may trim them or ask a vet to trim them – an operation that may have to be repeated periodically over the years. Surgical extraction of the tusks is not an option with most  pigs because the teeth are so deep-set within the lower jaw that the extraction would itself break or permanently damage the jaw. But *all* pigs have canines, and in some groups even the females' canines may grow outside the mouth and become tusks. However, if a male piglet is neutered, its canines may never grow enough to become full-sized tusks.

GROOMING FOR A SHOW

Y OUR PIG must be properly groomed before a show – which primarily means that you must wash the pig and clip the hair from the tail and the ears (especially the inside). The trotters must be clean, and there should be no dirt, mud or sawdust on the legs or back.

The equipment recommended for grooming a pig is:

* a hosepipe and running water (to wash the pig)
* waterproof boots (for you)
* a mild soap
* a largish scrubbing brush
* a soft nailbrush or smaller brush (for emergency/intricate cleaning)
* clippers (for clipping hair)
* rags (to use in washing and in drying)
* utensils that the pig recognises as containing food and drink.

PIG PERIODICALS

The *Pig Journal*, "the world's oldest pig journal", is published online by the UK Pig Veterinary Society, as hosted by ThePigSite.com. It is issued bi-annually in May and November and provides up-to-date articles and information on pig production, written by expert contributors.

However, the *PIG Newsletter* is published by the similarly UK-based (and internationally-oriented) Pipeline Industries Guild.

TAMING THE WILD BOAR

THE FIRST ATTEMPTS AT domestication of boars by humans are thought to have taken place between 10,000 and 8,000 years ago, probably originally near the Tigris in Mesopotamia. Historical authorities suggest that climatic conditions in that region then changed for the worse, causing those humans who relied for their livelihoods on boar-farming to migrate westward to Europe, where they were delighted to discover that not only were the climate and lifestyle better but also that European wild boars were easier to tame. It was only then that the metamorphosis of the bristly, dark-coloured wild boar into the comparatively short-haired, lighter-coloured domestic pig really took off – and considerably later still when separate varieties of pigs emerged as independent breeds. Even today, however, many piglets are born with much of the distinctive outer coloration of their wild boar ancestors.

THE PIGS OF ANIMAL FARM

The named pigs that feature in George Orwell's satirical novella *Animal Farm* (written 1942/1943, published 1945) are:

★ **Old Major** – a 12-year-old Middle white boar, probably largely based on Karl Marx and in the story a representative of ideal communism

★ **Napoleon** – a forceful Berkshire boar who becomes the leader of the farm animals and then a corrupt tyrant over them; he is based on Joseph Stalin

★ **Snowball** – an idealistic partner and then rival of Napoleon, eventually forced out by Napoleon and thereafter vilified as an enemy; he may be based largely on Leon Trotsky

★ **Squealer** – a small pig who is Napoleon's second-in-command and mouthpiece, the utterer of deceitful slogans and statistics; he would seem to be based on Vyacheslav Molotov (of "Molotov cocktail" fame)

★ **Minimus** – the bardic pig, composer of the second and third "national anthems" as the words of the first and second become politically inappropriate

★ **Pinkeye** – Napoleon's food-taster when he reaches the stage at which he believes he needs one.

SLIPPERY CUSTOMER

"Fame is like a shaved pig with a greased tail. It is only after it has slipped through the hands of some thousands that some fellow, by mere chance, holds on to it!"
DAVY CROCKETT (1786–1836), *US frontiersman, soldier and folk hero*

FEEDING YOUR PIG

FOR A FARM PIG TO GROW RAPIDLY and in good proportion it needs a high-energy, concentrated grain diet that is low in fibre – such as maize (corn), oats, wheat and barley – and is enhanced with protein and vitamin supplements. As the pig puts on weight, the quantity of additional dietary protein required also increases until a weight of around 56.7 kilograms (125 pounds) is achieved, at which point the diet should change to a less nutrient-dense regimen. Even more important to a pig's diet, however, is water. A pig should have as much pure clean water as it can drink.

VARAHA, AVATAR OF VISHNU

According to Hindu lore, the boar Varaha was the third of Vishnu's avatars. That is, the major god Vishnu took upon himself the form of the boar Varaha (whose name apparently *means* "boar", and which may or may not actually be etymologically akin to the English word) on the third occasion he assumed a different form in order to help humankind. This time it was to save the Earth from the demon Hiranyaksha who had dragged the Earth "to the bottom of the sea". And in this case, "the sea" is usually taken to mean "the cosmic ocean", but it may be relevant that Vishnu is scripturally described as "the ocean of all good qualities". Varaha defeated and killed the demon, and then arose from the "sea" bringing with him the Earth – generally portrayed as held between his boar tusks.

The Indian temple most famous for its connection with this story is in Sri Mushnam, Tamil Nadu. It is a site visited particularly by women desirous of child-bearing, who bathe in the Pushkarini Pool "in the shade of the banyan tree" while reciting a lengthy passage of appropriate scriptures, hopeful of going on to have many hardy children thereafter.

CAN PIGS SWIM?

They certainly can – and in emergencies, for long distances. There are several recorded instances of ships' pigs being torpedoed during World War II and swimming competently in deep sea water for some time until being rescued. In 1829 in northeastern Scotland, a number of piglets were overtaken by the flooding of the River Dee and apparently swam 8 kilometres (5 miles) before reaching safety. In all cases, the pigs seemed none the worse for their aquatic experience, refuting the common folklore which predicts that pigs that swim for any duration of time will inevitably cut their own throats with their sharp front trotters as they do so.

--------------- A PIG IN A POKE ---------------

To "buy a pig in a poke" is an English (and, as it happens, Swedish, Finnish and Estonian) expression meaning to "pay money for goods that may or may not be genuinely what you think you are buying". It derives from the late medieval practice of going to market to sell a piglet tightly enclosed in a poke basket or sack to stop it escaping. Unscrupulous traders might, however, substitute a comparatively valueless cat for the piglet – and a wary purchaser might therefore insist on seeing exactly what was in the poke bag before any money changed hands. In this case, if there was a cat inside, "the cat would be let out of the bag" – another, complementary, English (and, as it happens, German) expression – and the truth would be revealed.

Strangely, most other European languages (for example, French, Dutch, Russian, Polish, Danish and Latvian) confuse the two ideas, with the result that their idiom is to "buy a cat in the sack", by which they just mean that they are buying something that is quite possibly not really what they want.

--------------- THE BAY OF PIGS FIASCO ---------------

The Bay of Pigs (*Bahía de Cochinos*) is a wide inlet on the southern coast of Cuba some 150 kilometres (95 miles) southeast of the capital, Havana, which is on the northern coast. It is likely that in the English name for the bay, "pigs" is in fact a mistranslation for "triggerfish" anyway.

On 17 April 1961 – three months after the USA broke off diplomatic relations with Cuba following the Castro government's determined endeavours to nationalise all economic resources in the country, and some 15 months after the revolutionary coup that initially brought Fidel Castro to power – about 1,500 armed Cuban exiles resident in the USA landed in the Bay of Pigs. They seized the two beaches (Playa Girón and Playa Larga) at each end of the Bay, meeting little apparent opposition. Within three more days, however, the counter-coup was over, to the great bewilderment and humiliation of the US government and the CIA, which had sponsored, equipped and provisioned the attack.

HERALDIC PIGS

WILD BOARS – along with lions, eagles, bears and certain mythical creatures – are quite common on the coats of arms of families socially prominent in past centuries, and of historic cities and towns. It is much rarer to find families or urban centres so proud of their association with domestic pigs as to have one or more of *them* portrayed within their coat of arms – but there are a few. There is probably only one coat of arms, however, which depicts pigs in the heraldic position described as *rampant* – and that is the coat of arms belonging to what used to be the rural town of Sakkola in Karelian Finland, a town that since the end of World War II has been in Karelian Russia and is now instead called Gromovo.

SIMMERING QUIETLY

'If a pig loses its voice, does it become disgruntled?'
GEORGE CARLIN (1937–2008), US *comedian, author and critic*

EARS TO THE GROUND

"Pig's ear" is the common name both for a succulent plant native to South Africa otherwise known as the round-leaved navelwort (*Cotyledon orbiculata*) and for a type of edible mushroom otherwise known as the violet or clustered chanterelle (*Gomphus clavatus*). Neither of these organic growths bears any real resemblance to pigs' ears. The outer surface of the mushroom (which is known as the "pig's ear" also in German) is not unporcine to look at, but the shape is more a wider version of the standard chanterelle trumpet, and the navelwort's only possible excuse for its alternative common name (in English and Afrikaans) is that its leaves are wide and flap-like even if they are greyish green, and its pink flowers hang down in floppy bunches.

PIG SQUEALING CONTESTS

In rural France, contests for men to make as realistic pig sounds as possible – held at open show grounds and judged by pig-farmers (often also in the presence of live pigs in order to gauge any discernible effect on them) – are usually well attended. The contestants tend to dress up in pig masks, pinkish-grey overalls and pig-trotter slippers, and the winner's prize is generally a hamper of pork products.

SOW BY SOUTHWEST

Pigs seem to have an innate sense of direction. Adult pigs can find their way home across even unfamiliar territory from a comparatively long distance, despite the severe limitations of their visual ability.

PIGS OF THE NIGHT

THE STAR CLUSTER CALLED THE HYADES, in the constellation Taurus not far from its sister cluster, the Pleiades, has been called that since early ancient Greek times – a name that would appear to denote a connection with seasonal rainfall in Europe, apparently etymologically akin to the Greek verb *hyein* "[I] rain". (That same connection is why it is the Hyades that are referred to in the traditional English counting-song *Green Grow the Rushes-O* as the eight "April rainers".) But to the rural people of Italy during ancient Roman times, the Hyades were instead called Suculae, "the piglets". Pliny the Elder, writing in the first century AD, comments on this folkloric attribution, suggesting that because of the rains that caused such muddiness at this time of year, the stars in the cluster were delighting in wallowing in the mud like true pigs.

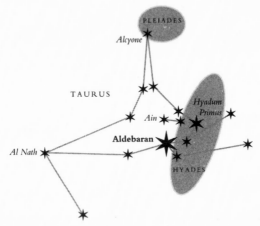

But this leads to another possible derivation for the name Hyades. If it has nothing to do, after all, with the Greek *hyein* "[I] rain", it very possibly could relate to the word that is now *hyena* in English and in most other languages – which specifically in origin (Greek *hyaina*) means "pig-like [animal]" and is etymologically akin to the (Germanic) English *swine*.

THE SWABIAN-HALL PIG BREED

THE SWABIAN-HALL PIG is large and described by farmers as "white" (by which they mean very light pink) with a black head and rear end, although the tips of the tail and the snout are "white" too. Between the black and "white" areas is a thin grey belt of pigmented skin beneath unpigmented hair. The *Schwäbisch Hällische Schwein*, as it is known to the Germans, is hardy, has a long lifespan, has high fertility (averaging 9.2 piglets per litter) and is generally a good mother with abundant milk. It is regarded by the Germans as one of their traditional pork-producing animals. Certainly, in the mid-19th century in the *Land* of Baden-Württemberg in southern Germany, and specifically in the area around the town of Schwäbisch Hall, these pigs were already famous and were being enthusiastically exported to other German-speaking countries. By 1959 no fewer than 90% of all pigs in Baden-Württemberg were Swabian-Halls. Yet, as abruptly as 25 years later, only eight Swabian-Hall purebred pigs were left there following a catastrophic attempt to improve the breed through nutritional regimes intended to increase body fat. Over the subsequent 25 years (to 2009), however, a remarkable turnaround took place. Deriving from those eight survivors there are now more than 1,500 Swabian-Hall pigs in their traditional area. Moreover, such is the excellence of the meat they produce that *Swäbisch-Hällisches Qualitätsschweinfleisch* (Swabian-Hall Quality Pork) is now a registered trademark and by order of the European Union an *appellation-controllée* (meaning that no pork from anywhere else may bear that prestigious name, just as Parma ham may come only from Parma in Italy).

LITTLE PIGS HAVE BIG TEETH

PIGLETS generally need their teeth trimmed ("clipped") because the piglets' canines are too sharp for the sow to bear when suckling, and the faces and legs of neighbouring piglets may also be torn and damaged, leading to a potentially fatal condition known as greasy pig disease/syndrome. The technical term for this is exudative epidermitis: a staphylococcal bacterial infection caused by bacteria that normally live on the skin but that invade roughened or damaged skin tissue and produce toxins that are absorbed into the system. On average 50% of suckling piglets that do get the disease will not survive. The sow may become reluctant to suckle and stop doing so. Nonetheless, teeth should not be clipped until at least six hours after birth, when the piglets have taken in sufficient quantities of colostrum (the mother's initial milk). Removing any part of the teeth earlier may predispose the piglets to inflammation of the joints.

──────── THE HOG OF THE HEDGEROWS ────────

THE HEDGEHOG — formerly also known in English as the hedgepig or furze-pig — is of course not a pig at all but a small mammal of the much older, nocturnally insectivorous order Erinaceomorpha and family Erinaceinae. Altogether, there are 17 different species belonging to five genera, native to Europe, Asia and Africa; the hedgehogs now all too common in New Zealand were introduced from Europe in the late 19th century. But if they are *not* pigs, why are they called "hogs"? Most people say that it is because they have a pig-like snout. The nose of a hedgehog, though sometimes longish, is, however, rather sharply pointed and nothing like the flattened snout of the domestic pig. The true answer is that we have forgotten how very bristly pigs used to be, as indeed wild boars still are, and it is the bristles or spines of the hedgehog that are referred to in the name — just as those spines are referred to in the word for the hedgehog in almost all major European languages, although only Norwegian (*piggsvin*), Danish (*pindsvin*), Icelandic (*broddgöltur*) and Hungarian (*sundisznó*) also use a term for a pig.

──────── TIPS FOR THE PIG SHOW RING ────────

❁ Enter the show ring as soon as your class is called.
❁ Be aware of where the judge is at all times.
❁ Use a small brush (that should otherwise be kept in your pocket) to remove any dirt, grease or dust that may get on your pig.
❁ Keep your pig between the judge and yourself, and around 3 to 4.5 metres (10 to 15 feet) away from the judge.
❁ Stay away from groups of people and other pigs: try to keep your pig moving freely where the judge can clearly see it.
❁ Look pleased with your pig.

──────── HAMM ────────

HAMM is one of the main secondary characters in the animated movies *Toy Story* (1995), *Toy Story 2* (1999) and *Toy Story 3* (2010) — in which children's toys and possessions come to life when there are no humans around. He is a talking, pink piggy-bank. Lively and often witty, he is a close friend of another main secondary character, Mr Potato Head. A version of Hamm also makes an appearance in the animated film *Cars* (2006), where he is a pink, piggy-bank-shaped armoured car. In all of these representations the voice of Hamm is supplied by the well-known actor John Ratzenberger.

PIGS IN THE PARK

IN AUGUST 2005 a German news agency reported on its website that over the preceding weeks and months the city of Berlin had been virtually under siege by some of the 7,000 or so wild pigs that were living in the woods surrounding the city. Their urban intrusions had caused devastation in gardens – vegetable gardens in particular had been despoiled – household pets had been terrorised to the point of refusing to go outdoors, and there had even been one or two shocking occasions where human residents and bellicose boars had confronted each other face-to-face. The agency called for action to be taken by the local council or indeed anybody who knew what to do and how to do it. The situation, it said, was intolerable.

The very next day, the news agency received an email reply to the effect that the situation was even worse where the email-sender was living, in that the intrusive pigs were undoubtedly bigger, more numerous and more ferocious. This respondent's home address was, perhaps inevitably, in Texas, USA.

THE BEARDED PIGS

There are two types of bearded pig: the Bornean (*Sus barbatus*) and the Palawan (*S. ahoenobarbus*). The former is of course a native of Borneo and a resident too of Sumatra and parts of Malaysia; the latter is a native of specific islands in the Philippines and only recently was proved not to be a subspecies of the former. Both types are indeed visibly bearded, in that they have lighter-coloured whiskers under the "chin", but they also have whiskers on top of the snout and so might be considered to be moustached as well. Borneans may also have a whiskery tassel or double tuft on the tail. In fact, the facial whiskers conceal a pair of warts on each cheek. The whole body tends to be longer and thinner than that of wild boars or domestic pigs, but despite that leanness, bearded pigs are preferred prey for the tigers and other large cats of their regions, and for that reason tend to forage and scavenge in close-knit family groups during the day.

Most of these groups regularly migrate once a year over considerable distances, at which time they travel by night and rest up in thickets during daylight hours.

Another unique property of these pigs is that they are able to jump at least their own height.

POINTLESS PRESENTS

'Don't give cherries to pigs or advice to fools.'
IRISH PROVERB

CHRISTMAS DINNER

IN SCANDINAVIAN COUNTRIES, the traditional Christmas dish is generally not turkey or goose but ham, and is eaten in the evening of Christmas Eve. This may well reflect the old Viking/Nordic custom of sacrificing a boar to the god Freyr at Yuletide in the hope that the god's blessing on the future year would be forthcoming as the days once more began to lengthen. When Christianity took over most of the old Viking traditions, much of the respect and ceremony previously afforded the god Freyr was transferred instead to St Stephen, whose feast day is 26 December. The apple that was once in the boar's mouth has since either become part of the salad dish that often precedes the main course, or been turned into the apple sauce that accompanies the ham.

FABLE: THE SOW, THE GOAT & THE SHEEP

A farmer gathered together a sow, a goat and a sheep from his farm, and put them into a donkey-drawn dray to take them to market. The goat and the sheep settled down peacefully for the journey in the dray, but the sow began to wail and scream and make a terrible noise, hardly stopping to draw breath. It went on and on. Eventually, the donkey couldn't take any more of it and, turning round in its harness, said to the sow: "Ssh, now! What's all the noise for? Why can't you be quiet like the others?" The sow replied, "The goat is being taken along for her milk. The sheep is with us for her wool. But what I am likely to have to contribute is something I may not be able to get back again!"

THE PIGTAIL

What in the 17th century was described in English (and some other languages) as a "pigtail" was a twist of tobacco. Over the next 150 years, however, it became almost solely the plaited pigtail of hair on young girls and – officially and formally, although then mostly described as a "queue" (via French from Latin *cauda* "tail") – of the contemporary (male) British army/Royal Navy standard "dress" for long hair. In the Navy, officers might wrap their pigtail in a linen bag, whereas ordinary seamen might smear tar over it – which is how the word "tar" became applied to ordinary seamen. Nonetheless, in a deliberately archaic fashion Robert Louis Stevenson refers to "pigtail tobacco" twice in *Treasure Island* (late 1870s). The resemblance of a (plaited) pigtail to the tail of a pig is chiefly in the way both types initially project out at right-angles from the backbone/scalp before curving or twisting down.

THE EVEN-TOED UNGULATE

A PIG HAS four toes on each foot, and even then walks on only the middle two, which are specially extended and larger, so forming the so-called "cloven hoof" of the even-toed ungulates. The tips of the hoof toes are the equivalent of nails, and are accordingly very hard and sharp-edged, although when rooting for food the pig uses the generally even harder but much more malleable and sensitive edge of its snout. The smaller toes, which appear one each side a little above and behind the hoof toes, are of little practical use but may on occasion be brought into play when scrambling down or up a steep slope. Perhaps to balance the fact that the pig really only uses two toes to stand on, the heel bone is surprisingly large, extending some length behind the "ankle".

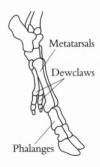

Metatarsals

Dewclaws

Phalanges

PIGS ON THE WING

The progressive rock group Pink Floyd issued the album *Animals* – to some acclaim and a certain amount of controversy – in 1977. It begins and ends with the song *Pigs on the Wing* that is split into two halves, sandwiching three other long tracks – *Dogs*, *Pigs (Three Different Ones)* and *Sheep* – all sung by writer Roger Waters accompanying himself on acoustic guitar.

In an interview around 15 years after the album's release, Roger Waters strongly implied that *Pigs on the Wing* was written as a declaration of love for Carolyne, his partner of the time. Critics have noted, however, that whereas the second half of the song does indeed have a positive theme of reciprocated love and care, the first half is, at best, tentative in spirit, halfway towards the genuine negativity expressed in the other three tracks which all apparently refer to types of people to avoid if possible. The expression "pigs on the wing" derives, after all, from a World War II fighter pilot's warning to others that enemy planes were approaching from the blindspot.

PIGFEED ADDITIVES

Most foodstuffs given to pigs naturally and inevitably contain bacteria. When feed is stored for any length of time before being fed to the pigs, the bacteria in it may greatly increase in both number and potential toxicity. Antibacterial compounds may therefore be added to the feed and, by reducing the bacterial uptake, enhance the growth of the pigs while making the feed more economical to provide. Note, however, that all medications in feed must be withdrawn for the government-regulated number of weeks before a pig is sent for slaughter.

HOT & BOTHERED

PERHAPS BECAUSE PIGS evolved as creatures of the forest, rooting around the tree trunks where the sun rarely penetrated, they are prone to suffer from the effects of heat. Those effects are especially marked in relation to the pig's reproductive system. For sows, heat stress can cause the postponement of oestrus (regular sexual preparedness) and miscarriage (stillbirth) or abortion. The first week and the last two weeks of pregnancy are critical, but it is almost as important to protect a sow from high temperatures during the second to fourth weeks of pregnancy, around the time of birth, and through the lactating (nursing) period immediately after the birth. For boars, heat stress causes the death of sperm cells, resulting in up to seven weeks of infertility following the incidence of the high temperature. Moreover, if the air temperature reaches 40°C (105°F) and above, a boar loses all interest in sexual activity until the temperature is lower again.

CIRCE TURNS ODYSSEUS'S MEN INTO SWINE

The enchantress Circe (ancient Greek *Kirkē* "falcon"), daughter of the sun god Helios and the sea-nymph Perse, according to Homer in the *Odyssey*, lived on the island of Aeaea (thought now to be the rocky promontory on the west coast of central Italy currently named Monte Circeo). Odysseus (Ulysses) and his small fleet called in there to restock with supplies and were invited for a meal with the enchantress. Most of the crews went, leaving Odysseus and a few men back at the ships on guard. The food and drink they consumed was strange but pleasant and abundant – and was spiked with a strong drug. All but one wary crew member succumbed. He ran back to tell Odysseus, who ventured out at once to rescue his men. The god Hermes accosted him on the way, advising him to swallow some of a sacred herb named *molu* (in some translations called "holy moly" and now thought possibly to represent a snowdrop)

which would counteract Circe's drug, and enable him to force Circe to restore his men to their senses. He arrived at Circe's palace to find that his crews had to a man been turned into pigs. But the sacred herb worked as Hermes had said it would, and Odysseus duly obliged Circe to restore the men not only to their senses but to their proper shape. They all stayed with Circe for a further year, feasting and drinking, before resuming their interrupted voyage. Not long afterwards, Circe gave birth to Odysseus's son Telegonus, later to become ruler of the Etruscans.

———————— THE FOUR SOW GODDESSES OF NEPAL ————————

Guarding the gates of cities, temples and sacred shrines in Nepal are the four sow deities Vajravarahi (the red guardian of the west, protector of livestock), Nilavarahi (blue guardian of the east), Swetavarahi (also called Sukarasya, guardian of the south) and Dhumbarahi (grey guardian of the north, protector of humans against the disease cholera). In their names, the element *-varah-* or *-barah-* means "boar", and all are depicted as boar-headed, although Swetavarahi's alternative name Sukarasya actually means "face of a sow".

———————————— PIGS & BRONCHITIS ————————————

Pigs have small lungs in relation to their body size, and for that reason are particularly susceptible to respiratory diseases and disorders, such as influenza, pneumonia and bronchitis, the latter two of which may be quickly fatal to a pig. There is no suggestion that humans can catch bronchitis from pigs – as they can swine flu – yet a 2006 study in Finland established that bronchial diseases and disorders were on average twice as common among pig farmers than among the (human) population in general. This is regarded as a "work-related condition" and probably has much to do with manual labour amid sawdust, grain dust, dirt and soiled straw in feeding and mucking out the pigs. Furthermore, residual damage that caused respiratory difficulties was evidently not relieved when pig farmers retired or changed job but in fact tended to become worse than if they had continued working with pigs.

———————————— THE PIG'S SENSE OF SMELL ————————————

THE FLAT-FRONTED NOSE (snout) of a pig is largely cartilage that contains a multitude of nerve filaments and is well supplied by the bloodstream, beneath thin, very tactile skin that has far fewer hairs on it than on the rest of the body. The result is an extreme sensitivity both to touch and smell, made good use of by pigs in the wild, which have to root out their food from the ground surface beneath overgrowth and foliage, and sometimes even beneath the ground surface itself (as with rooting out truffles – a pig specialism made good use of by human owners in many countries of Europe). The snout is so sensitive it has been suggested that it contains as many touch receptors as humans have on both hands. And as for smell, the pigs' sensitivity is held to be greater even than that of dogs – although of course the fact is that pigs have to rely on the sense of smell even more than dogs do, since their sight is so relatively poor.

HOGS ON ICE

The hog score or hog line is a technical term in the sport of curling, corresponding to either of two lines across the ice 6.4 metres (21 feet) from each tee (the line across the centre of the concentric circles known as "the house").

Hog line   *Hog line*   *Tee line*

               72ft   21ft
              21.95m   6.4m

At the playing end, the first hog line is the line by which a stone must be released, and at the target end the second hog line represents the least distance at which a stone may come to rest and still remain in the game. If a stone fails to reach the second hog line, it is removed from the ice playing area (the curling sheet). Formerly, such a stone was described as a hog because it "hogged" the view of the target for the next player. Now a stone which is removed for that reason is instead said to be "hogged" off the ice.

HAM & THE HAMBURGER

THE "HAM" in the name of the German city of Hamburg probably has little or nothing to do with the ham that goes with salad or in a sandwich, let alone the "ham" that is the supposed filling in the eponymous hamburger (which classically is chopped and reshaped beef). But, there is a small possibility that the site of the original early ninth-century settlement, which was on a rocky mound within a marsh between the rivers Elbe and Alster, did visibly suggest a human thigh with a rounded buttock at one end. This is the definition of the word *ham*, which is of Germanic origin, and which is also the derivation of the term for the cold pork meat. German historians insist that the first element of the city's name is of obscure etymology – although other authorities contend that the original name Hammaburg represents no more than the *burg*, "stronghold", of the *hamma*, which equates to the English *ham* as in "hamlet" – in which ham means "settlement" and is cognate with the word *home*.

THE DISDAINFUL SNOUT

'A pig used to dirt turns up its nose at rice.'
JAPANESE PROVERB

BLOOD PRESSURE & HEART RATE

The normal systolic blood pressure of an adult pig (and a cat) is statistically averaged at 128mm of mercury (whereas the standard adult human – and dog – blood pressure is around 120mm of mercury). The average heart rate of an adult pig is 70 beats per minute (human 60, dog 90, cat 150). The average lifespan for a pig living a relatively stress-free life is reckoned to be 25 years (human 70, cat and dog 15), resulting in a total number of heartbeats for that lifetime of 92 million (human 2.2 billion, cat 1.18 billion and dog 71 million). To take the pulse of a pig, find the prominent artery at the base of an ear or under the tail.

SADDLEBACKS

THE SADDLEBACK BREED OF PIG originated as a combination of two other English breeds: the Essex and the Wessex (both named after the areas to which they were native). The breed is best known for a distinctive, lighter-coloured hoop or belt around a darker-coloured body – representing the "saddle" from which of course it partly gets its name. The hoop or belt varies greatly both in width and in colour definition between individual pigs, even pigs from the same litter, strongly implying that the marking is not genetically specific. The pig's ears droop around the face. A hardy pig well suited to an outdoor lifestyle and with good grazing characteristics, the saddleback has been used worldwide for cross-breeding purposes to improve the stock of other light-coloured breeds. This has the added advantage of passing on the saddleback sow's potential as an excellent mother, giving birth to large litters and having abundant milk.

THE THREE LITTLE PIGS

The nursery story of the Three Little Pigs was first published in the 1840s, although it dates from at least two centuries earlier. Basically, the tale tells how each of the three made a house for itself. The houses of the first two pigs were built of feeble materials and were easily destroyed by the Big Bad Wolf, who then ate the pigs. The third pig's house was made of brick, however, and the only way the wolf could gain access was down the chimney – at the foot of which the wily pig had placed a cauldron of boiling water. The wolf thus met its own end, and was duly eaten by the pig. This story has since been greatly tamed, not least in the Walt Disney cartoon version of 1933 in which none of the pigs is eaten and the wolf is simply humiliated and punished.

─────── THE PIG OF THE CHINESE ZODIAC ───────

The Chinese zodiac corresponds to an overall 60-year cycle made up of five repeating segments of 12 years, each year of which is named after one of the zodiacal animals. The 12 animals involved have nothing to do with constellations or other astronomical entities but simply represent supposed personality types based on the human characteristics associated in folklore with the animals. The first animal in the Chinese zodiac is the rat – and the twelfth and last is the pig or boar (in language and culture the Chinese do not distinguish between the two). Additionally associated with the zodiacal pig/boar is the element water (the other zodiacal elements being wood, fire and metal; the fifth Chinese element, earth, does not feature as a zodiacal aspect) and the disposition *yin* (the female, darker, colder principle of the philosophical dualism complementary to *yang*). In Chinese culture, the pig is primarily linked with the traits of fertility and virility, and these qualities are reflected in the highly positive personal qualities of (physical and mental) growth and strength associated with the zodiacal pig/boar. However, it should be pointed out that the Chinese do *not* believe that everyone born in the same year must have much the same personality: there are further zodiacal aspects of personality related to the month and to the time of day when birth occurred, both governed by the same 12 zodiacal animals. Aspects of pig/boar personality may therefore be found also in people who were not born during a Year of the Pig, and people who *were* born in such a year may have aspects of personality linked with other zodiacal animals.

─────────── NOSE RINGS ───────────

Pig rings are not completely circular but are attached to the outside edges of the snout, rather than through the nostrils. Many comprise about three-quarters of a ring, although another common type looks something like an inverted figure 3. They are almost always clipped on – no surgery or piercing is involved. The rings are generally made of thickish copper wire about 2.5 centimetres (1 inch) in diameter, with conical or even triangularly pointed ends. Often, more than one ring is fitted to a pig because rings can become dislodged and fall off: a particularly active adult pig may be fitted with as many as four. The whole purpose of fitting a ring is to stop a pig from rooting into and through the ground surface. Rooting behaviour is made impossible with a ring because the snout can no longer be pressed into the ground. Continuing to try is likely to cause the pig pain – and it is for this reason that the practice of fitting rings remains potentially controversial. Some pig-farmers never fit rings. Ideally, of course, pigs may be kept in an environment in which preventing them from their natural rooting behaviour is unnecessary anyway.

——— THE LUCKY PIG MUSEUM, BAD WIMPFEN———

Bad Wimpfen – a spa town on the River Neckar in south central Germany, some 70 kilometres (46 miles) north of Stuttgart – is rather off the beaten track for tourists despite its scenic location and historic buildings. Perhaps accordingly, it contains a surprising number of somewhat eclectic museums including, for instance, what the town's civic brochure describes as "the Guardian Angel Museum" and (more to the point) "the Lucky Pig Museum". The latter displays no fewer than 14,000 exhibits in the form of ceramic pigs, glass pigs, plastic pigs, carved wooden pigs, metallic pigs, stone pig statuettes, paintings, drawings and etchings of pigs, pig documents and certificates, and other eye-catching porcabilia. Models and copies of some of the exhibits are available on sale in the museum shop. The museum is currently open daily from April to the end of October, but at weekends only from November to the end of March.

——— UNDER ATTACK ———

Pigs can harbour a wide range of parasites that cause diseases – diseases that may in turn be transmitted to humans, including:

✱ **TRICHINOSIS**: infestation of muscle tissue by larvae of the nematode worm *Trichinella spiralis*
✱ **TAENIASIS**: infestation of the intestine by the pork tapeworm (*Taenia solium*)
✱ **CYSTICERCOSIS**: parasitic infestation of the entire central nervous system following ingestion of the eggs of the pork tapeworm (*Taenia solium*)
✱ **ASCARIASIS**: infestation of the intestine by one or more nematode roundworms of *Ascaris* sp.

The relatively common incidence of these parasites in pigs is a central reason always to maintain scrupulous hygiene when handling or approaching pigs, and always to properly cook or cure pork meat before eating.

——— JUMPING PIGS ———

The world record height ever jumped by a pig is 70 centimetres (27½ inches), a feat performed by a pot-bellied pig named Kotetsu ("Little Iron One") on 22 August 2004 and listed formally in the *Guinness Book of Records* of the following year. The event took place at the Mokumoku Tedsukuri Farm in the Mie Prefecture on Honshu island, Japan.

THE SPINY PIG

THE PORCUPINE is another animal of which the English name evidently has something to do with pigs – and indeed the name does come from medieval French *porc d'épine* "spiny pig" – although of course the porcupine is a large rodent (actually, the third largest altogether, after the capybara and the beaver). In all, there are 27 species belonging not just to different genera but to two quite separate families, Histricidae (native to the Old World) and Erezithontidae (native to the New World). Many languages other than French and English seem also to reckon the porcupine to be a spiny pig including Spanish *puerco espín*, Italian *porcospino*, Portuguese *porco-espinho*, German

Stachelschwein, Dutch *stekelvarken* and Finnish *piikki-sika*. This is possibly not only because of its size but also because it makes excellent eating – once all the quills have been removed of course. In some other languages (notably Hebrew and Swahili), the word for "porcupine" is the same as the word for "hedgehog".

TIRPITZ

In the first decades of the 20th century, pigs were often kept on board naval ships so that the crew could eat fresh meat. One such pig, a young male, was on the German Imperial Navy cruiser *Dresden* in November 1914 when the ship took part in the Battle of Coronel, off the coast of central Chile, and in the Battle of the Falkland Islands a month later in the South Atlantic. The second battle was a defeat for the German fleet, but the *Dresden* managed to escape, and tried to hide from two British pursuit vessels in Cumberland Bay, off what is now known as Robinson Crusoe Island, Chile. However, the British ships – HMS *Glasgow* and HMS *Kent* – tracked the *Dresden* to its lair, and the German crew, seeing that capture was inevitable, thereupon scuttled the ship. The pig went down with it. But

unlike the ship, it bobbed up to the surface again, where it began swimming. Perhaps an hour later the pig was approaching HMS *Glasgow*, where it was spotted in the water by one of the petty officers who, somewhat surprisingly, jumped overboard and swam to the pig to rescue it. With some difficulty, the rescue was effected: the pig was brought aboard, immediately made the ship's mascot, and named Tirpitz (after the German admiral and Secretary of State). Tirpitz remained aboard HMS *Glasgow* for a year, until the ship docked back in its home port in England again. After a period in quarantine, he was transferred – together with the petty officer who had first rescued him – to the naval gunnery school at Portsmouth, in the grounds of which he spent the remaining four years of his life.

───── THE FABLE OF THE HARE & THE PIG ─────

A fable related by the Indian thinker Ramaswami Raju tells how a hare and a pig agreed to have a competition to see who could best jump over a ditch. It was quite a wide ditch and presented a challenging hurdle, but both contestants were keen to put their heart into clearing it, as if by doing so each proved that he was somehow the superior animal. The contest duly took place – the hare went first. He leapt, and soared through the air . . . but came down just short of the further edge of the ditch, tumbling back and down into it. Then it was the pig's turn. He leapt as high and as far as he could . . . but landed right in the middle of the ditch. Both animals were disappointed – but still felt that the contest needed a decision between them. They asked a fox who had been watching to tell them who had done better, and which was thus the superior animal. "Well," said the fox, "the contest was to jump over the ditch. You both failed to do it. I can't say that either of you was better than the other."

───── IF MUSIC BE THE SWILL OF LOVE ... ─────

It was reported in 2007 that a Vietnamese pig farmer had begun to play recordings of the symphonies and concertos of Beethoven, Mozart and Schubert to encourage his pig workers as they tended the 3,000 pigs on his pig farm. However, he was delighted to discover that the pigs seemed to be reacting to the music – by eating more and gaining weight faster. No information is available on whether the pig workers ate more and also put on weight.

───── KUNE KUNES ─────

KUNE KUNE PIGS are native to New Zealand, although they seem to have descended from Asian pigs that were introduced to the country in the early 19th century by whalers or seafaring traders, and were then adopted and developed by the indigenous Maori people. *Kune* – pronounced "coony" – is the Maori word for "rotund", and the repetition of the term merely adds emphasis. The pigs certainly are well built (some descriptions actually use the word "dumpy"), are very hairy and tend to have a fringe of loose skin (a wattle) hanging from the lower jaw. They come in a wide variety of colours and colour combinations from pink to gold to brown, sometimes also with black or dark blue areas. Because they are particularly friendly towards humans, they are now often treated as household pets. Since the 1970s – a decade in which purebred kune kunes came close to extinction – a breeding recovery programme has seen an extraordinary increase in numbers and an extension of the pigs' popularity elsewhere in the world, notably in Wales.

---------------------- CHORIZO ----------------------

Chorizo is the Spanish word for several types of pork sausage that originated either in Spain or in Portugal, and that are generally fermented, cured and smoked and then eaten in cold slices. (There are, however, some varieties that are sold "fresh" – that is, raw – and have to be cooked before being eaten.) Spanish and Portuguese chorizo is typically a deep red or red-brown colour, due to the high content of dried, smoked red peppers within the mixture of salted chopped pork and pork fat. Spanish chorizo contains additional garlic and herbs and may be more or less smoked, according to local custom. Portuguese chorizo (*chouriço*) may include wine and paprika and other seasonings, sometimes also affecting the overall colour. The chorizo produced in the former Portuguese colonial territory of Goa, in India, is much hotter and spicier than the European types. Mexican varieties include a chorizo that is actually green in colour.

---------------------- BLADDER PROBLEMS ----------------------

From the 16th to the 19th centuries, pig's bladders from slaughtered pigs were used much in the same way that balloons and footballs are used today. However, when appropriately inflated in those days, they were almost as light and fragile as balloons are now, and since they were generally not cured or otherwise treated after removal from the pig, most of them were also serious health hazards. Sixteenth-century jesters must frequently have had to renew the bladder at the end of their wands. Late 18th-century public schools in England must have used up five or six airily floating "balls" in any single game of what passed for football. It was only at the beginning of the 19th century that a leather covering was put over the pig's bladder before it was inflated, and the football became a much heavier item which thereafter spent most of its time on or near the ground. But because pigs' bladders were not standardised in size or shape – some when inflated were more oval than round – the balls were similarly diverse, even when covered in leather. And that is how the (eventually regulated) difference between a soccer ball and a rugby football arose.

LAMB ON PORK

'Pig – let me speak his praise – is no less provocative of the appetite, than he is satisfactory to the criticalness of the palate. The strong man may batten on him, and the weakling refuseth not his mild juices.'
CHARLES LAMB (1775–1834), *English author, essayist and gourmand*

PIG CHROMOSOMES

HUMANS ORDINARILY have 46 chromosomes in their body cell nuclei. Some may have one or two fewer or one or two more, but such differences very often (though not always) manifest themselves in some kind of physical and/or mental deficiency or deformity. The wild boar (*Sus scrofa*) ordinarily has 36 chromosomes . . . but the domestic pig that was bred from it actually has 38 – which might explain why the domestic pig is different in characteristic ways from the wild boar. Or it might do nothing of the kind, for if a difference of two chromosomes could be held to represent a change from "wild" to "domestic", what does that suggest of the relationship between humans with 46 chromosomes and chimpanzees (a closely related species) with their 48?

ROOTING & RINGING

Pigs have a wide streak of curiosity and are forever rooting around with their snouts, turning things over and looking under objects to see what is there – especially if it might be food. This behaviour is generally fine for a pig that is kept outdoors and that has its own ark or shelter from the wind and rain. But if a pig is kept indoors and the floor surface (even under straw) is concrete or stone, the pig may all too soon damage its snout by trying to root through it. A nose ring may be urgently required to stop it from doing so.

Moreover, even when a pig lives outdoors and is allowed to roam on relatively open land, if that land does not belong to the pig farmer but is common land (on which such a licence for pigs to roam is technically known as pannage), a nose ring is required again so that no permanent damage results to the common land through its natural rooting behaviour.

BLODWYN PIG

BLODWYN PIG was a blues-rock/progressive rock group founded and led by guitarist Mick Abrahams (formerly of the group Jethro Tull) in 1968. The group's most famous album was *Ahead Rings Out* (1969), the cover of which featured a pig's head wearing headphones and dark glasses, a ring through the snout, and smoking something that looked like a cigarette. Over the 1970s and 1980s the group broke up and reformed several  times, only seriously coming together again for specific periods in the 1990s to produce three more albums, none of them particularly successful, but one of which was called *Pig-in-the-Middle* (1996).

PIGGING OUT

Pigs evolved primarily to take advantage of the grasses that made their appearance in the early Eocene epoch. Their digestive system adapted accordingly, and although they continued to have just a single stomach – whereas some other artiodactyls (such as cattle) grew multiple stomachs – that single stomach was strengthened and toughened, to the extent that it was not just grasses that pigs could eat but quite a number of other things besides. They became omnivores. Today, in the wild, pigs go foraging, still eating grass where they find it but also taking in flowers, foliage, roots and fruits, some of which they may dig up with their snouts. Yet they will also eat tree bark, dead insects, worms and the rotting carcases of dead rodents and other small animals. Worse, in moments of high stress (and particularly when they feel confined and restricted) they may eat their own young and other pigs.

THE HUNTING OF TWRCH TRWYTH

Welsh forms of the legend of King Arthur include *The Hunting of Twrch Trwyth*, in which Twrch Trwyth is a magical boar that carried a comb, scissors and a razor in the hair between its ears. The animal is often now described as female because in the story it tended to live and travel with seven boar piglets – but this is to ignore another part of the same story which told how the boar had once been a prince and had been turned into a boar as a permanent punishment for his many undescribed but evidently heinous sins. The seven piglets had been his male companions and had undergone a virtually identical metamorphosis. In Welsh, *twrch* means "hog" (and not specifically "boar") and it is thought that *trwyth* is an adjective meaning precisely "changed", "altered by infusion", in reference to the former prince's changed state and status. The reason for the presence of the comb, scissors and razor is that these implements were said to be desired by the giant Ysbaddaden because they were the only ones capable of cutting his hair. Obtaining them was a condition set the hero Culhwch – whose name, incidentally, means "pig stick", and who was a cousin of King Arthur – in order to gain the hand of the giant's daughter, Olwen of the white footprints.

A PIG GOES "OINK"

Well, no, it doesn't. A pig squeals, shrieks or grunts rather than genuinely oinking. A donkey oinks more realistically. But the classic sound a pig makes has nonetheless long been said in English (and apparently in German, in Spanish, in Portuguese and in one or two other languages) to be "oink".

———————————— IN A PIG'S EAR ————————————

The hearing of most pigs is excellent but non-directional. Although in human terms pigs' ears are generally large, the external parts of each ear do not focus sound into the hearing apparatus as human ears do, with the result that a pig can hear a noise as well as a human can, but may not necessarily know where the sound is coming from – which, if the sound is unusual or apparently close, may cause the pig to stop dead and hold its breath until it finds out what it is. Conversely, pigs are quick to remember noises that are non-threatening and commonplace and and that can safely be ignored.

———————— THE BOAR'S HEAD CELEBRATION ————————

THE BOAR'S HEAD CAROL is a world-famous piece of church music first published by the Alsace-born London printer Jan Wynkyn de Worde in 1521 in his *Christmasse Carolles*. Musically, it is effectively a kind of 16th-century ecclesiastical chant, of which the first words (in the original) were:

> *'The bores heed in hand bear I,*
> *With garlands gay and rosemary.'*

The carol is still annually sung in the refectory (dining hall) of Queen's College, Oxford, England, on Christmas Day, when a roast boar's head is ceremonially brought in and eaten by all present. The eating of a boar's head at Christmas was, in medieval times, intended to symbolise the triumphant overwhelming of sin (represented by the joyful consumption of an animal acknowledged to be the most dangerous likely to be confronted by ordinary people) through the birth of Christ.

An annual boar's head festival is still observed at several other locations in England, Canada and the USA, most famously perhaps in Christ Church Cathedral, Cincinnati, Ohio, where a parade is held every Christmas involving many parishioners, musicians and actors.

———————————— PSEUDO-RABIES ————————————

PSEUDO-RABIES is a relatively common viral disease among pigs world-wide, although in Western countries vaccination programmes have been remarkably successful, in some areas achieving near-eradication. The virus involved is porcine herpesvirus 1, and is spread by oral or nasal contact. Adult pigs who catch it generally show no symptoms at all, but in piglets and exceptional adult cases there may be severe and eventually fatal complications. Unhappily, other farm animals such as cattle, cats and dogs may contract the virus and subsequently suffer rabies-like symptoms (hence the name of the disease) followed fairly rapidly by death. Humans appear to be immune.

PORCINE PARADISE

"Like a pig in clover" is an English simile that is recorded from the end of the 18th century, but probably dates from very much earlier, usually meaning "as happy as a pig given free rein to gorge on its favourite food". That clover (*Trifolium* sp) is indeed a favourite food of pigs is well known. In fact, a scientific test in the USA in 2005 proved that pigs overwhelmingly devoured white clover (*Trifolium repens*) in preference to a whole collection of other supposedly much-enjoyed plant foods. So much so in fact that the pigs, once they had finished off the white clover in the bed specially prepared for the test, laid waste to the bed itself, overturning the soil, rooting through it and trampling it, hoping to find more clover. From the 1880s the USA was probably the first country in the world to establish the cultivation of entire fields of clover specifically as fodder for pigs. Yet in the USA a different connotation of "like a pig in clover" is that the pig might be surrounded by *too much* of a good thing – and would inevitably waste some.

PIG, KENTUCKY

Pig, Edmonson County, central Kentucky, USA (elevation 225 metres (733 feet)), is a small "unincorporated community" – meaning that it is more a place on the map than a regular township, although it is the site of the local landmark that is the Pig Diner and does apparently also have its own cemetery. It stands at a crossroads on the KY 259 Brownsville Road that represents the junction of KY 422 Pig Road, which comes up from the southwest, and the National Park Boundary Road, which strikes off northeast towards the nearby Mammoth Cave National Park. Pig lies some 27 kilometres (16 miles) northeast of Bowling Green, the principal city of the Metropolitan Statistical Area in which Pig is situated.

THE STUTTERING STAR

Porky Pig is a world-famous animated cartoon pig that since his first appearance in March 1935 (as a supporting character in *I Haven't Got a Hat*) has retained extraordinary popularity in the Looney Tunes and Merrie Melodies series produced by Warner Bros. His trademark stutter – featured particularly in his standard line at the end of Looney Tunes shorts, "Th-th-th-that's all, folks!" – may have come about solely through the fact that the actor first chosen to voice the role (Joe Dougherty) stammered helplessly. Porky's name was reportedly derived from the nickname of a childhood friend of the original 1930s director, Fritz Freleng.

BORDERLINE VISION

PIGS are thought generally to see in two dimensions, not three, although the sight from two eyes ought to produce stereoscopic vision over the 50 degrees of visual overlap forwards. This dimensional restriction occurs because the retinal elements that enable the distinction of borders and boundaries by human eyes are much weaker in pigs, and borders and boundaries therefore probably appear as ghostly gradations of different colours, chiefly red, green and blue. Without borders and boundaries there cannot be any real sense of depth or distance although the pig presumably learns to interpret some degree of depth and distance in what it sees. When spectral gradations occur in reality (as in a rainbow), the pig is unable to see them because the gradations between gradations cancel each other out.

Because the pig cannot ordinarily interpret what it sees in more than two dimensions, and because borders and boundaries that are difficult to interpret occur increasingly from the pig's eyeline upwards, the pig feels safer when the view above its eyeline is neutral or single-coloured or has spectral gradations that from the pig's viewpoint render the view neutral. Conversely, a major factor in stress for pigs is an environment that is moving or changing, and the higher (more upwards) the changes appear (as when something approaches more closely from a distance), the greater the stress for the pig.

THE BRITISH LOP

The pig breed known in the UK as the lop, and outside the UK generally as the British lop, was internationally established in 1920 but has ever since been largely restricted to southwestern England, notably the county of Devon. Its comparative and continuing rarity is difficult to explain in the light of the pig's normally amiable disposition, its ability to graze and to thrive with little specialised care, and its excellent health record. It is a biggish pig, usually described as "white" (which in its case often means greyish yellow), with long and fine white hair and large, thin ears that hang well down over the face.

Those ears probably account for its name, as in the other descriptive English expressions "lop-eared" and "lopsided". And it is perhaps such connotations that in turn have persuaded lop owners to concentrate less on improving the breed and more on sending their lops to pig shows and exhibitions.

THE SIGN OF THE PIG

In Chinese astrology, the pig is one of the most honourable signs of the zodiac. People born under that sign are held to be generous but perfectionists, delighting in the good things of life and wanting the people close to them to enjoy those things too. They tend to think only the best of others, and will put up with physical and mental discomfort if necessary to hold on to that view. They may thus be easy to take advantage of – but once disillusioned, they can be vicious and unforgiving enemies who enjoy taking revenge with intelligence and refinement appropriate to their perfectionist lifestyle. Yet, in general, happiness for themselves and for others is the ultimate goal of those born under the sign of the pig.

LET SLEEPING HOGS LIE

Pigs tend to use daylight as their main reference to the timing of sleep – they "make their bed" or "rearrange their nest" as dusk falls, slumber through the hours of darkness, and wake up at the dawning of the new day. On the other hand, pigs are perfectly happy to take a nap at any time of the day if they feel disposed to do so, and especially during summer when the nights are shorter anyway. As for whether pigs snore: piglets usually don't, adult pigs certainly may and fat adults generally do. Pigs are also known to dream.

LEATHER FORECAST

P IG LEATHER – produced in the same way as leather from cattle – remains popular among the manufacturers of belts, wallets, briefcases, handbags, boots and shoes. The general public, however, is not ordinarily aware of which type of leather is used, although it is said to be just possible to distinguish between pig leather and cattle leather with the naked eye because the "grain" of pig leather contains far fewer tiny, pore-like holes where the hair has come through the skin surface. Unexpectedly, leather of an altogether superior quality is obtainable also from the hide of the pig's close relative, the peccary – the wild pig of the Americas – and is used in fine leather products, especially luxury shoes, jackets and gloves, because of its durability, suppleness and extra imperviousness to water.

SEND IN THE CLONES

Scientists in March 2000 reported the birth of the first five cloned piglets. Their names were given as Millie, Christa, Alexis, Carrel . . . and Dotcom.

THE PIGGY BANK

Ceramic piggy banks, now fairly common worldwide, seem to have been an English invention of the late 18th century – although small ceramic models of buildings into which coins were inserted for saving were used by the ancient Greeks, and ordinary wooden or metal money boxes were relatively common in the far-flung colonies of ancient Rome. But in England, the piggy bank evolved into its customary form through something of an etymological misunderstanding, for the original version was just a jar made out of rough clay – and it was the clay that was known as *pygg*. With coins inside it, the clay jar was thus a "pygg bank".

Many countries now make a range of piggy banks, most of which in their own languages are called the equivalent of "pig money boxes" (e.g. French *cochon tirelire*, Spanish *hucha de cerdito* and Polish *świnka-skarbonka*) or "savings pigs" (e.g. German *Sparschwein*, and Danish/Norwegian *sparegris*).

SIZE MATTERS

Pigs have definite preferences when it comes to how they eat and drink, and thrive only when these preferences are deferred to in the arrangements made in their pens. They need enough left-and-right space to get their heads into a trough, and they need the trough and any water pipeline to be at the correct height for them above the ground. Both these requirements depend on the pigs' shoulder width and shoulder height – and both these measurements can be calculated as a statistical average from a pig's weight. Farmers wishing to make the appropriate arrangements in a pig pen may thus use the following table (initially worked out by Dr Jim Bruce at the Centre of Rural Buildings in Scotland during the 1980s).

WEIGHT		SHOULDER WIDTH		SHOULDER HEIGHT	
KG	LB	CM	IN	CM	IN
5	11.023	10.9	4.29	27.2	10.71
10	22.046	13.7	5.39	34.2	13.46
20	44.092	17.2	6.77	43.0	16.93
30	66.138	19.7	7.76	49.2	19.37
40	88.184	21.6	8.50	54.1	21.30
50	110.230	23.3	9.17	58.2	22.91
60	132.276	24.7	9.88	61.8	24.33
70	154.322	26.0	10.24	65.0	25.59
80	176.368	27.2	10.71	67.9	26.73
90	198.414	28.3	11.14	70.6	27.80
100	220.460	29.3	11.53	73.1	28.78
110	242.506	30.2	11.89	75.5	29.72
120	264.552	31.1	12.24	77.7	30.59
130	286.598	31.9	12.56	79.7	31.38

THE EARTH PIG

THE AARDVARK — *Orycteropus afer*, the sole member of its genus and the sole extant member of the ancient (and otherwise extinct) family Tubulidentata — is of course not a pig, but the first Dutch settlers in what is now South Africa thought that with its rather hairy body, its wide ears and its long snout-like nose it looked something like one. They called it an "earth pig" (modern Dutch *aardvarken*, modern Afrikaans *erdvark*) partly for that reason and partly because it does actually burrow down into the earth to make its lair to rest in during the daylight hours. At night time it emerges to go on forays, sometimes for long distances, to ravage ants' and termites' nests, licking up the insects in vast numbers with its extraordinarily long, sticky tongue. A few languages other than English (e.g. Italian and Portuguese) use the word *aardvark* for the animal, but the majority translate it as "earth pig" (e.g. Icelandic *jarðsvín*, Danish/Norwegian/Swedish *jordsvin*, German *Erdferkel* ["-piglet"], French *cochon de terre*, Polish *prosię ziemne*, Finnish *maa-sika* and Turkish *yer-domuzu*), the Spanish describing it instead as an "anthill pig": *cerdo hormiguero*.

PIG RACING

Pig racing — which involves getting piglets to run around a short track made of cinder, gravel or Astroturf in apparent competition with each other, often additionally jumping over small hurdles or fences — is a form of entertainment that is almost entirely restricted to the USA but that occurs on a very occasional basis also in the UK and Australia. Such races are generally organised as supporting events, as novelty attractions held before or to one side of a principal sporting occasion, county fair or other form of public show that features livestock. Novelty entertainment or not, the piglets when racing usually wear greyhound-style numbered jackets as if a form-book was being kept, although they are evidently too intelligent to need a "hare" to chase after.

BUDDY, CAN YOU SPARE $56,000?

The world's most expensive pig was called "Bud" — which may or may not have had anything to do with the fact that the man who bought him for $56,000 in March 1985 was also called Bud. That Bud Olson made the purchase together with a partner, Phil Bonzio, from one Jeffrey Roemisch of Hermleigh, Texas, is not in doubt. But why they should have paid that huge sum for a young, male, neutered cross-breed pig is simply not recorded.

─────── THE FABLE OF THE CAMEL & THE PIG ───────

The Indian thinker Ramaswami Raju tells of an argument between a camel and a pig. The camel began by saying, "It is much better to be tall than to be short. I am tall, and I can tell you." To which the pig replied, "On the contrary, it is much better to be short than to be tall. I am short, and I know." The camel looked down its nose at the pig and said, "Well, I believe I can prove that being tall is better – and if I can't, I will give up my hump." The pig gazed shortsightedly up at the camel and retorted, "Fair enough. If I can't prove that being short is better, I shall give up my snout." "Do we agree on that, then?" asked the camel. "Absolutely," affirmed the pig.

They walked along together and came to a garden enclosed by a low wall in which no gate was visible. The camel bent its neck over the wall and made a hearty meal of the plants and foliage in the garden, while the pig trotted around the wall looking vainly for a way in. Finished, the camel turned to the pig and said mockingly, "*Now* don't you think that being tall is better?"

They walked on further and came to another garden – one enclosed by a very high wall in which there was just a low opening at one end. The pig made its way through the opening and found beds full of the most delectable vegetables, while the camel in turn strode round the outside of the wall, not able even to see over it. Replete, the pig came out again and said pointedly to the camel, "*Now* don't you think that being short is better?"

But the more they thought about it, the more they came to the joint conclusion that the camel should keep its hump and the pig its snout – for being tall is better sometimes, and being short is better sometimes: they both have their own benefits and advantages in the appropriate circumstances.

───────────────── THE PIG GENOME ─────────────────

IN NOVEMBER 2009 it was announced that the international collaboration between scientists to decode the genome sequence of the domestic pig was all but complete, with just 2% left still to unravel. The research was undertaken on DNA taken from a red-haired Duroc pig belonging to the University of Illinois, USA, but the sequencing work was carried out by scientists all over the world under the overall aegis of the Wellcome Trust Sanger Institute. Although the full sequence is not yet completely known, the results of the research have been published as they were discovered, and various significant conclusions are said already to have been reached. Genes that might be used to assist in the improvement of pork production and meat quality have already been pinpointed. But more significantly still, the full sequence when available is expected to contribute to a better understanding of some human diseases and disorders, in particular to the treatment of some serious cardiovascular, pulmonary, gastrointestinal and immunological conditions.

————————————— LUNCHEON MEAT —————————————

"LUNCHEON MEAT" is the current UK supermarket term for a type of cold meat that comprises between 60 and 80% pork, together with water and pork fat and various spices, and is sold sliced (as if) from a sausage or meat loaf to be eaten cold with salads or in sandwiches. However, in international terms – and particularly in relation to EU terminology – "luncheon meat" is just one of the descriptions of *any* kind of meat that is precooked and served cold on trays or plates, or with bread, otherwise known as cold cuts. They include all varieties of ham and salami – and similar cuts of cold beef and lamb.

————————————— PRISCILLA & HER FAMILY —————————————

Priscilla was the name of a much-celebrated pig who in late July 1984 saved a mentally retarded boy named Anthony Melton when he got out of his depth and was in serious danger of drowning in Lake Somerville, Houston, Texas, USA. The boy managed to hang on to the pet pig's collar and leash as she swam for shore, where his horrified mother was waiting. Four years later, one of Priscilla's offspring – apparently called Jeffrey Jerome – was formally (and with fully applied legal constraints) expelled from Houston to symbolise the plight of all homeless citizens of the city. His name thereafter featured in advertisements and leaflets as that of the principal money-raiser for the cause.

————————————— HYBRID —————————————

T HE ENGLISH word "hybrid" derives from Latin *hybrida*: "piglet that is the result of the mating of a wild boar and a domesticated sow". It is because of this original contrast between two essentially different natures (wild and domesticated) and the fact that a third party (the owner of the sow) is potentially responsible for their forceful if not enforced union that the word has – particularly in agricultural and horticultural development – come primarily to mean a cross-breed between two distinctly different types of related organism, especially one that is the result of human intervention. Other languages that use variants of the original Latin word to mean the same as the English word include French, Spanish, Portuguese, Dutch, Norwegian, Swedish, Russian, Polish, Serbo-Croat, Finnish and Turkish. This list does not, however, include Greek – from the ancient form of which language the Romans actually derived their own word *hybrida*. That is because in ancient Greek the original word combined two word-elements that together described simply the violent coming together of two different dispositions, with the result that derivatives in modern Greek have connotations only of verbal abuse and physical injury.

THE JITTERY PECCARY

Peccaries are a sort of smallish wild boar native to the Americas from the far southwestern states of the USA southwards. There are four species, all of which belong to the family Tayassuidae – the collared peccary (*Pecari tajacu*, also known as the musk hog or skunk pig), the white-lipped peccary (*Tayassu pecari*), the giant peccary (*Pecari maximus*) and the Chacoan peccary (*Catagonus wagneri*) – generally located from north to south. Their aggressive nature means they cannot be domesticated, although some groups of collared peccaries live in urban areas and endeavour to ignore humans altogether as they devour their vegetable gardens. All peccaries tend to live in herds that observe some forms of social behaviour, notably the scent marking of group territories. Herds can be dangerous to other animals, including humans, especially in group defence, for which they make formidable use of their short, straight tusks.

TRANSPORK

MOVING PIGS around is always stressful for the animals – and pigs under stress tend to stop still, prick up their ears, sniff and refuse to go a step further (sometimes also holding their breath) until they feel reassured enough to move on. This means that getting a single pig to move perhaps only 18 metres (60 feet) from one pen to another can take an excruciating amount of time if the pig is not familiar with the smell, sound and sight (in that order) of the surroundings. And moving more than one pig at a time can take disproportionately longer still. That is why it is generally advised that pigs be moved in groups of no more than seven, preferably less.

HOGGING THE STAGE

The Three Little Pigs is a 40-minute opera for schoolchildren by John Davies (2010), based on the music of Mozart's most popular operas and with a storyline familiar to most children thanks to Disney cartoon animations or equivalents. Thus the pigs Don Giovanni and Cherubino build their houses of sticks and straw, whereas their sister Despina visits the library to study "huff-proof puff-proof" house construction before building her own house in that exemplary fashion. The villainous Wolfgang Bigbad thereupon blows down Despina's brothers' flimsy residences, the brothers duly seek refuge with their much more sensible literary sister – and the opera (unlike the aforesaid villainous Wolfgang Bigbad) has the appropriately happy ending.

THE PIGNUT

THE PIGNUT (*Conopodium majus*), also called the hognut, the earthnut and the earth chestnut, is a plant native to northern and western Europe and coastal North Africa. An umbelliferous plant featuring clusters of small, white flowers on thin stems branching from a single long stem, it has narrow leaves that are deeply divided. The English name "pignut", though, comes from the small, brown, rounded tuber that is its root, which grows not far beneath the soil surface and which was therefore a popular food for pigs in the days when the animals used to roam freely through shaded undergrowth in woodland. In fact, the tuber – the "nut" of the pignut – is edible for humans too, raw or cooked, once the thin layer of brown skin has been peeled off. Folklore in Ireland suggests that the pignut is a favourite food of leprechauns. Much less daintily, folklore in Scotland apparently decrees that eating a surfeit of pignuts leads to an immediate and catastrophic infestation of head lice. In France, the animal associated with the pignut is not the pig but the brown bear, which is surprising because bears never were particularly numerous in France and in their present, very restricted area up in the Pyrenees mountains are currently in danger of extinction.

The greater pignut (*Bunium bulbocastanum*) is, as its name suggests, larger but similar in shape. It is from the same plant family (Apiaceae), but is of a different genus and has a different preferred habitat. Known alternatively as black cumin, it is native to an area from southeastern Europe to southern Asia.

———————————— THE ARTICULATE PIG ————————————

Because of their good hearing ability and relatively poor vision, pigs have over the process of evolution developed a very basic "language" of vocalisation calls with which to communicate with each other. Piglets squeak, grunt, squeal and bark, and older pigs use a variety of grunts (oinks) and squeals in order to indicate hunger, thirst, alarm, fear, affection, sexual desire and many other emotions. In terms of volume, a pig can squeal so loudly (up to a measured 112 decibels) as to permanently damage the hearing of any human too close by – yet pigs visibly appreciate being spoken to softly by humans.

———————————— SET UP, SET DOWN ————————————

IN ANCIENT EGYPT, Set (or Seth, Sati, Sut or Sutekh) was the sun and daylight god who was the primary deity of the Hyksos, those strange, warlike invaders from the north-eastern Mediterranean coastlands who first entered Egypt in about 1800 BC. They ruled the nation as military overlords between about 1650 and 1540 BC, but were finally expelled, all traces of their presence being immediately expunged from records and monuments by the restored native pharaohs. In form, the god Set was depicted as (or closely associated with) a big black boar. Following the downfall of the Hyksos, pigs and the people who worked with pigs were regarded by the Egyptians as disgraced, unworthy and even dirty. Swineherds were, for example, no longer allowed to participate in public worship of the other deities. Some element of this abhorrence of pigs is likely to have contributed to the dietary laws against eating pig flesh to this day upheld by Judaism and Islam. Meanwhile, the god Set was redefined as the lord of the powers of evil, whose chief assistant was the serpent Apep, and his name became that of Shaitan, the Islamic name for the Devil (regarded as meaning "adversary" or "enemy"), better known in biblical English as Satan.

———————————— SWINE BRUCELLOSIS ————————————

SWINE BRUCELLOSIS is a highly contagious bacterial disease in pigs. The bacterium involved is *Brucella suis* and is spread through contact with any body fluid except saliva. Symptoms include inflammation of the joints and sex organs, abscesses, lameness and partial paralysis. There is no effective treatment for the disease, and no vaccine to prevent it. It is possible for humans to contract the disease through contact with infected body fluids or by ingesting contaminated meat. For this reason *Brucella suis* was in 1949 selected by the US Army's Chemical Corps as its first standardised biological agent for use as a chemical weapon.

MAKING A PIG'S EAR OF IT

In English, "to make a pig's ear of" something is to complete it very badly – the implication being that the ear of a pig is its most worthless part, the part that is least well shaped. It has been suggested, however, that this expression is in fact derived from lead smelting in the 18th and 19th centuries. Boxes, especially strongboxes, were made of, or lined with, lead, and were sometimes made by casting a lead base and then adding the sides and finally the lid. If things went wrong in the second and third stages, the sides and lid might overheat and fuse together, distorting into a sort of leaf-shaped flap not altogether unlike the shape of a pig's ear. And so the lead worker would have made a pig's ear out of what was meant to be a box.

THE MARINE PIG

THE MARINE MAMMAL known in English as the porpoise has for millennia been compared – at least linguistically – with the pig, for in the Latin of ancient Rome the porpoise was *porcus pisces* "the pig fish". In medieval French this became *porpeis* – and thus *porpoise* in English. However, in many of the languages of northern and western Europe the idea of the "marine swine" is expressed not with reference to Latin but to Scandinavian Germanic – Danish *mar-svin* – thus apparently giving rise to modern French *marsouin*, Portuguese *marsuínos*, and Polish *morświn*, whereas the Russians have simply translated it in full as *morskaya svinina* (specifically "sea pig"). Other such translations include the German *Meerschwein* or *Schweinswale* ("pig whale") and the Irish Gaelic *muc mhara* ("pig of the sea"). Even in South American Spanish the porpoise is the *chancho mariono*, the "marine pig".

PIGS & MUCK

The island of Muck in Scotland (*muc* is "pig" in Scottish Gaelic) is one of the Small Isles (with R[h]um, Eigg and Canna), 3.2 kilometres (2 miles) long by 1.6 kilometres (1 mile) wide. Its population in 2009 was 38 (from 144 in 1764 and 68 in 1841). It is administered as part of Inverness-shire; there is one road and electricity is supplied by the island's two wind turbines (which are not part of the national grid), backed up when there is no wind by a diesel generator. The one small school currently educates seven pupils, although pupils aged over 12 are obliged to go to boarding school in Mallaig on the mainland. In any case the main schoolroom is used on Sundays for religious services because there is no church. Visitors/tourists are discouraged from bringing motor vehicles onto the island although a ferry service that would facilitate this was inaugurated in 2007. Instead, visitors are encouraged to bring their bicycles.

THE 1976 SWINE FLU SCARE

The celebrated swine flu scares of 1998 and 2009 were by no means the first. The swine flu announced in 1976 as likely to become epidemic among humans caused considerable panic in the USA. There was an almighty rush to be vaccinated. In the event, the epidemic did not materialise – a total of only 13 cases were in fact recorded in the USA, and just one death. However, 535 of the many thousands of people who had been vaccinated developed Guillain-Barré syndrome, a normally rare condition involving potentially lethal paralysis, and 25 of them died.

PRESIDENTIAL INSIGHT

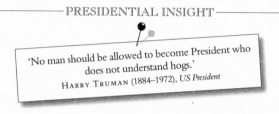

'No man should be allowed to become President who does not understand hogs.'
HARRY TRUMAN (1884–1972), *US President*

PEPPA PIG

Peppa Pig is an animated TV series devised and produced by Astley Baker Davies (that is, Neville Astley, Mark Baker and Phil Davies) and E1 Entertainment, screened as a young children's show consisting of combined five-minute episodes. Each episode represents a scene from the daily life of Peppa, a two-dimensional, five-year-old girl piglet portrayed as if living the lifestyle of a real human five-year-old girl. Peppa thus lives with her Mummy and Daddy and her baby brother George in a house at the top of a hill. She has an extended family (Grandpa Pig, Granny Pig, Auntie Pig, Uncle Pig, etc.) and a multitude of friends, many of whom live with their respective families (such as Richard Rabbit, Rebecca Rabbit, Ruby Rabbit; Suzy Sheep – Peppa's best friend – and Sarrion Sheep; Danny Dog and Deedee Dog; Zoe Zebra; Candy Cat; Pedro Pony; and so forth). The full "cast list" numbers well over 60. The screening of the first series of 52 five-minute episodes began in the UK (on Five) at the end of May 2004. Its first transmission in the USA (on Cartoon Network) was in August 2005 and, two months later, one episode was awarded the "crystal" for Best TV Production at the Annecy Animated Film Festival. The latest series is the third (first broadcast May 2009). The programme, dubbed in the appropriate languages, is shown in many countries of the world, including China. Peppa's name also changes according to language – in German she is Peppa Wutz, in Welsh Peppa Pinc, in Finnish Pipsa Possu and in Danish Gurli Gris.

THE TAMWORTH TWO

T HE TAMWORTH TWO was the name given by the UK press to two Tamworth Ginger piglets who escaped while being unloaded from the transport vehicle at an abattoir in Malmesbury, Wiltshire, England on 8 January 1998. The five-month-old pigs squeezed through a perimeter fence, swam across the River Avon and disappeared into the back gardens of a nearby residential area, apparently heading north. Pursuers could find no trace of them. Their escape caused a media sensation. Despite the fact that the piglets were one male and one female, they were nicknamed Butch and Sundance after the celebrated (male) US outlaws. TV crews from around the world (particularly from the USA and Japan) descended upon the area, filming everything that moved. Helicopters crammed with reporters and cameramen crisscrossed the Wiltshire sky. The UK press, apparently following the lead of the *Daily Mail*, set up a campaign to ensure that the pigs, once they were captured, would not be reconsigned to the abattoir. But for a week, no one saw anything at all of them.

Then they were both spotted one evening raiding the vegetable garden of a couple whose house backed on to a dense thicket on the side of a hill at Tetbury, Gloucestershire, some 5.6 kilometres (3½ miles) north-northwest of Malmesbury. Trained staff were summoned, and Butch – the female piglet – was cornered and captured. Sundance, however, evaded all attempts to hold him, and made it back into the thicket where it was evident that the pair had been lying low. But it was now known where he was, and the next morning he was driven from his hiding-place by a man with two springer spaniels, immediately shot with a tranquilliser gun, and taken to a vet's to recover.

Courtesy of the *Daily Mail*, the Tamworth Two were spared the abattoir and have instead spent the rest of their lives to date as pampered inmates of an animal sanctuary at Ashford, Kent. Their former exploits were further celebrated by the release of a movie entitled *The Legend of the Tamworth Two* in April 2004.

THE GROUNDHOG

What in the USA is ordinarily called a groundhog (or a woodchuck or occasionally a whistlepig) is in fact a type of short-tailed ground squirrel or marmot (*Marmota monax*) that tends to live at lower altitudes than other marmots. Groundhogs have since the 1960s featured in the highly spurious but much celebrated festival of Groundhog Day on 2 February every year, in which the appearance (or not) of a wild groundhog at a certain location is held to forecast the beginning of spring (or not). The movie *Groundhog Day* (1993) centres on such a festival at Punxsutawney, Pennsylvania – at which the prophetic groundhog is known as Punxsutawney Phil.

———————— THE FABLE OF THE WOLF & THE PIG ————————

A wolf was making his way back home somewhat ponderously after having eaten and drunk his fill at an enormous feast that was attended by many different animals. Turning a corner, he came across a pig eating some swill, and stopped to rest his legs and take a breather. The pig looked up and exclaimed, "You do look tired! What have you been doing, wolf?" The wolf replied, "I'm on my way home from the huge feast that the lion presided over. But surely you know this, pig – weren't you there too?" The pig looked down again, and asked rather wistfully, "Were there many nice things to eat, many fine dishes?" "Oh yes, there certainly were – many wonderful dishes, and all beautifully prepared," said the wolf. Rather more eagerly, the pig asked again, "Was there swill to eat? And chaff?" Appalled, the wolf cried out, "Of course not, you silly animal! Swill and chaff at a feast? Heaven forfend!"

One person's feast is another's recipe for gastronomic hell.

———————————————— WILD BOARS ————————————————

Wild boars mostly live in scrubby woodland where there is plenty of leafy ground cover. There they can eat fungi, tubers, nuts and green vegetation, but they may also find carrion, small animals and reptiles to eat. Females and young male boars (up to four years old) usually live in groups of between 20 and 30, travelling and eating overnight from sundown to dawn, sometimes covering a considerable distance but with resting periods. Socially, such groups rely on the presence of one dominant female. Adult males live solitary lives, sometimes digging burrows for themselves, but come together in mid-Autumn to compete ferociously for the right to mate with females.

———————————————— LONG PIG ————————————————

"LONG PIG" is the English translation of the Polynesian term for human flesh cooked and eaten as meat, as ghoulishly reported by explorers and travellers in the islands of the South Pacific during the last decade of the 19th century and the first decades of the 20th. It was at this time that stories of cannibalism by exotic savages were particularly popular among schoolboy readers in north-western Europe who might themselves one day grow up to become colonial officials in such far-flung territories. The major implication of the term "long pig" is that human flesh, when cooking or cooked, smells and tastes like pork. And indeed, it *is* a well-established scientific fact that porcine body tissues are physically so similar to human tissues that pig organs can sometimes be used, partly or wholly, temporarily or permanently, to replace defective or missing human body parts in transplant surgery.

A PIGBOAT

"Pigboat" is a US slang term for a naval submarine in dock alongside others (because the submarines aligned side by side look like piglets feeding from their mother).

---WITCHCRAFT & MAGIC IN CELTIC MYTH---

CERIDWEN (or Cerridwen or Cereduin) is the name of one form of the ancient Welsh (Celtic) mother goddess, associated through her name both with a magic cauldron and with the wisdom and decrepitude of old age. In either case, her major attribute is a facility with witchcraft and the ability accordingly to change her shape into virtually anything. One of the shapes that she took most often caused her to be known alternatively as "the Old White Sow". It is possible that the word "white" in this nickname also bears some reference to her connection – as a mother goddess and patroness of the female reproductive system – with the moon. But whiteness was also associated in Welsh myth with death and the pallor of corpses, and it was as a white sow that Ceridwen was sometimes supposed also to devour the dead. Her magic cauldron was moreover a symbol of the Underworld, from the unfathomably dark depths of which nonetheless sprang inspiration and divine knowledge.

It was a similar connection with the cycle of life and death (and another magic cauldron) that the Irish/Scottish sea deity Manannán mac Lir – known to the Welsh as Manawydan fab Llyr – was held to possess a herd of magic pigs on whose flesh the gods feasted in the evening, only for the pigs to regenerate over the next 12 hours to be ready for eating again the following evening.

---PORKOPOLIS---

Cincinnati, in Ohio, USA, was in the 19th and early 20th centuries often known as "Porkopolis" because, as the western USA was opened up to agriculture, the city was the major focus of pork processing and packing at the centre of a huge area of pig-farming.

———THE PIG AS ENVIRONMENTAL HAZARD———

The main environmental issues related to pig farming are to do with pollution of local water supplies and pollution of the atmosphere. Water pollution most commonly comes about through insufficient management and ineffective disposal of pig manure, in which the pollutant chemical elements of most concern are nitrogen and phosphorus, although organic effluents and pathogenic toxins may be present as well. Pollution of the atmosphere centres on the emission of ammonia (again mainly from ineffective disposal of manure) and of greenhouse gases, particularly methane and nitrous oxide. In general, with respect to pigs, however, atmospheric pollution is far less significant than water pollution, and is ordinarily a case of no more than locally unpleasant odour. Environmental health and safety agencies in most countries publish national maps of areas at risk from both forms of pollution – information that is available also on their websites.

———THE DECORATIVE PIG———

THE CELEBRATED WEMYSS WARE (Griselda Hill) Pottery, based in Fife, Scotland, issues no fewer than 34 ceramic pigs with different designs on them, in a total of three different sizes, and some in limited editions. The pigs are mostly for decorative purposes only, but some are alternatively available in the form of piggy banks. Under different managements, Wemyss Ware has been produced in Fife (and occasionally elsewhere) since 1850 and has always featured brightly painted pigs, rabbits and cats as major design elements, sometimes additionally on plates, bowls and jugs. Wemyss Ware products old and new are regarded as highly collectible, and are priced by makers, dealers and auctioneers accordingly.

———FARROWING CRATES———

Throughout the pig-farming industry since the early 1990s, selective breeding for lean, fast-growing pigs has caused a surprisingly large increase in overall size of the adult sow. Moreover, the more birth episodes (parities) a sow goes through, the larger she tends to become anyway. Consequently, it has been formally noted in the industry literature that the standard farrowing crates (the strong frames in which sows are put to give birth) that were of sufficient length 20 years ago – in the UK, a 2.1-metre (7-foot) crate – are now hopelessly inadequate and may even cause permanent injury to sows if retained in use. Currently recommended instead are 2.4-metre (8-foot) crates, and it is stressed that this increased length is intended to be a measure of the available space within the crate, and should not include troughs or rails within the outer frame.

THE GRINDING LEGAL PROCESS

"Litigation: a machine which you go into as a pig and which you come out of as a sausage."
AMBROSE BIERCE (1842–1914[?]), *US satirical journalist and short-story writer*

THE HEALING PIG

Powdered extract of pig's bladder was reported in 2007 to have remarkable – almost miraculous – healing properties. Lee Spievack was working in a hobby shop in Cincinnati, Ohio, USA in 2005 when he put his right middle finger too close to a model airplane's whirling propeller and abruptly lost about a centimetre (⅖ inch) off the end, at an angle such that a bit of the nailbed remained. His doctor advised a skin graft and told him he would never regain the full use of the finger – but Mr Spievack's brother Alan was a medical research scientist who had been experimenting with powdered pig's bladder extract as part of a treatment to repair torn ligaments in horses. Lee thereupon applied the powder every two days. He claims that within four weeks the fingertip had completely regrown, and in a further three months the blood and nerve supply were apparently normal. Further experimentation on the use of pig's bladder extract to heal wounds and restore body parts is said since to have been taking place with the sponsorship of the Pentagon. However, there have also since been continuing and severe criticisms by high-ranking medical scientists all over the world as to the veracity of the original story.

MINE'S LONGER THAN YOURS

The longest unsmoked sausage prior to 2010 was made in Turija, Serbia, in February 2009. It was unofficially measured at 2.025 kilometres (1 mile 454 yards) long. Organisers said that they planned to produce a sausage at least 1 centimetre (⅖ inch) longer every year. The longest *smoked* sausage was made in Bucharest, Romania, in December 2008. Officially measured at only one-seventh of the length of the Serbian sausage, it nonetheless weighed 150 kilograms (330 pounds), and was chopped up, cooked and devoured with great gusto by the witnessing city populace.

MAD HOGS & ENGLISHMEN

SUNBURN is a problem for pigs, especially sows. Prevention is by far the better option than treatment after the event. Methods of prevention include providing shelter from harsh sun, and making sure that there are wallows in which pigs may cool and cover themselves with some sunscreen equivalent. Brassica tops – such as parsnips and turnips – in the diet should be avoided because they are said to predispose some pigs to sunburn. When sunburn occurs, however, the symptoms as in humans are a reddening and eventual blistering of the skin surface, with considerable pain. Severe sunburn can lead to skin eruptions with oozing of serum and a real possibility of secondary bacterial infection. Any subsequent fever may cause temporary disruption of a pig's reproductive system – serious enough in a pregnant sow to cause abortion. Treatment for lesser forms of sunburn in pigs, on the other hand, is much the same as for humans: get them to stay indoors or under shelter as much as possible, and use a body lotion and aloe vera (but not an oil, because an oil surface in further sun would actually increase the sunburn). If the pigs are unwilling or unable to wallow in mud (perhaps because the wallow is out in the sunshine), smear the pigs' bodies with mud yourself – a layer of mud will enable the skin to heal more quickly, feel cool for a time and prevent flies from pestering. More serious sunburn conditions involving skin lesions require wound dressing and/or the application of antibiotic powder. If necessary, administer pain relief food supplements.

THE PIGTAIL MACAQUE

There are two almost indistinguishable species of the pigtail macaque monkey (*Macaca nemestrina*) native to all lands from India east to western China and south to Malaysia and Indonesia. They are so called because their short, almost hairless tail does indeed have the classic form of a pigtail.

SONG OF PIG

Song of Pig is the somewhat sparsely translated title of a Chinese song freely available on the Internet, written and sung by Xiang Xiang (real name Wang Jinmei, born June 1984). Possibly the most listened-to song in the history of the world to date, it is said to have been downloaded well over a billion times in Chinese-speaking areas of the world, turning its creator into a pop idol and becoming the title track of her first album (February 2005).

HEAVY THINKER

THE AVERAGE WEIGHT of the brain of an average adult pig has been calculated at 180 grams (6.35 ounces). This compares well with the brain weight of an average sheep (140 grams (4.94 ounces)), medium-sized dog (72 grams (2.54 ounces)), cat (30 grams (1.06 ounce)) and rabbit (12 grams (0.42 ounce)), but is not so impressive against the brain weight of an average cow (440 grams (15.52 ounces)), horse (530 grams (1 pound 2.7 ounces)) or camel (762 grams (1 pound 10.9 ounces)), much less of an adult human (1.350 kilogram (almost 3 pounds)). But of course the overall weight of the brain also corresponds to some extent with the overall size and weight of the animal involved – and need have little to do with intelligence.

JUST TEETHING

Just as in humans, the first set of teeth in pigs comprises "milk teeth", also called deciduous teeth, which eventually loosen and fall out to be replaced by the final or permanent set of teeth. In humans, this is a fairly long-drawn-out process that happens mostly between the ages of six and 12. In pigs, however, the process takes much less time – perhaps three months or so – when the pig is around 1½ years old, by which time it is fully sexually mature.

THE BOAR OF CALYDON

From the time of Homer, several ancient Greek authors described the great hunt that took place to rid the city-state of Calydon of a monstrous boar sent by the goddess Artemis to ravage the area. Artemis had been enraged when the city-state's king, Oineus, had forgotten to pay tribute to her when making offerings to the other major deities, and the destructive depredations wrought by the boar were her revenge. Oineus was therefore obliged to hastily summon all the best hunters available, including Theseus, Castor and Pollux, Jason (the leader of the Argonauts), Iphicles and Atalanta, and send them out under the direction of his own son Meleager to try to trap and kill the boar. The hunt was successful in its primary aim – the boar was duly despatched, though not before it killed a few of the hunters – but the ramifications afterwards were

disastrous. There was violent disagreement over who should be considered the best hunter and thus take the largest share of the spoils, notably the boar's skin, and the quarrel soon escalated, first into murderous combat between individuals and then into outright war between factions and finally between entire city-states. Oineus' son Meleager was one of the first to die. Artemis had her revenge.

———————— BECOMING FAMILIAR ————————

Pigs were occasionally thought in medieval England to be witches' familiars, perhaps because a pig was a relatively unusual household companion for an old woman who lived alone and looked after herself, and who was thus open to hostile suspicions of being a witch. (It was actually far more common for a cat, a dog or even a rat, to be considered a witch's familiar.) Besides, a pig tended to root around in the topsoil and dig things up, suggesting to the gullible a connection with the diabolical powers of the underworld. And because a familiar was regarded as an intermediary that a witch might send to attack a disliked person, a potentially dangerous animal like a pig would also fit the bill. Yet according to extant records, there is only recorded case in England in which a pig was actually held to be a familiar. In Northamptonshire, in the 1720s, the said pig was described as being used as a (strictly terrestrial) form of transport, to carry three witches on its back at the same time to visit one of their sick friends.

———————— ZINC DEFICIENCY ————————

A disorder in pigs caused by a deficiency of the mineral zinc in the diet is not common – most commercial pig feeds contain a well-balanced selection of minerals and other nutrients – but does sometimes occur in young piglets before they are weaned. Initial signs are a thickening of the skin in reddish circles on the belly, which then spread to the legs, forward to the head and backward to the rump. The circles then become scaly and dry, and start cracking and splitting; then the hair falls out. Treatment for the condition is simply to make sure that an appropriate quantity of zinc is included in the food supplied.

———————— POSITION IN THE HIERARCHY ————————

Pigs are social creatures and rely on a strict and stable hierarchy within their groups, the hierarchy changing only as a group changes, and as new members have to establish (or be taught) their level within the group. A pig's first encounter with the social hierarchy occurs at birth, among its littermates, in the competition for its mother's teats. The piglets that suck on the first pair of teats will put on more weight than those who suck on other teats – and will be the dominant piglets of the litter. The hierarchy from top to bottom of the litter according to teat order is defined within 48 hours of birth and within seven days is not only stable but applied in respects other than just nourishment – reinforced when necessary by biting and kicking the piglets of lesser status. The teat-order hierarchy may remain in force even after the piglets have been weaned, although this generally happens only if the litter stays together and is not mixed with piglets of other litters.

─────────────── PIG HILL ───────────────

Swindon, in the English county of Wiltshire, is a large town known in the UK mainly for pioneering a type of traffic roundabout comprising a series of mini-roundabouts surrounding a larger one, and otherwise for being a typical, grey, industrial urban centre (official motto *Salubritas et Industria*, "health and industriousness")

just off a major motorway. Outside the UK, however, Swindon is perhaps most notable (as of 2010) for being – astoundingly – twinned with the Disney World theme park in Florida, USA. Evidently, nobody made the Disney executives aware of the etymology of the name Swindon: Old English *swīn dūn*:"pig hill".

─────────────── A PRIVATE FUNCTION ───────────────

A Private Function was an award-winning British comedy film starring Michael Palin, Maggie Smith and a first-class cast, released in November 1984 and shown at the 1985 Cannes Film Festival. The plot revolves around the measures taken by local businessmen of a northern English town in 1947 to evade the severe restrictions of contemporary food rationing after World War II, and to celebrate the wedding of Princess Elizabeth and Philip Mountbatten by secretly rearing a pig to eat on the occasion. A government food inspector, responsible for maintaining the rationing restrictions in the area, gets wind of the scheme and attempts to foil it, but things become even more complicated when the pig is stolen – and has to be concealed as best as possible – by Gilbert Chilvers (Michael Palin) and his wife (Maggie Smith).

Three six-month-old female pigs all called Betty were used in making the film, on at least one occasion becoming so stressed as to represent a potential hazard to actors, film crew, props and scenery.

─────────────── A PIG'S IQ ───────────────

According to world-famous US behavioural biologist Edward O. Wilson, the order of animal IQ (after humans, which is number 1) is:

2 *Apes*	4 *Certain types of whale*	6 *Elephants*
3 *Some monkeys*	5 *Dolphins*	7 *Pigs*

This would seem to justify the pigs' reputation for being pretty clever in comparison with most other animals – but this is to judge IQs from a solely human viewpoint, relating to what *we* deem to be clever or not. Moreover, since the IQs of humans differ so greatly anyway (very few people are credited with the notional average IQ of 100), it is quite likely that the IQs of pigs also differ greatly, and therefore possible that the pigs tested for their IQs to date may all have been particularly clever or, equally, particularly clueless.

THE DUROC STRAIN

THE DUROC STRAIN of characteristically red pig comes from the USA, but its ancestors were originally imported there from elsewhere. Some say they arrived with Columbus, De Soto and other pioneers from southwestern Europe, others say they came from the Guinea coast of Africa together with slaves. However, it would seem likely that there is a connection also with the red Berkshire hogs imported from England into Connecticut by the 1830s (before the red colour was entirely bred out of Berkshires between the mid-19th and early 20th centuries). In time, and from those early decades of the 19th century in the USA, two distinct strains of red pigs gradually merged into one breed, the strains being known respectively as Durocs and Jersey Reds. Slightly smaller than the Jersey Reds, the Durocs were given that name in honour of a famous thoroughbred stallion of the 1820s that was stabled at a farm on which some of the red pigs were also kept. Current Duroc pigs may range in colour from a pale gold to a very deep purplish red, but a medium dark red is the most common and regarded as standard. The pigs have a slight concavity of the face, over which the ears partly droop. They also have a reputation for being extremely aggressive – and for yielding exceptional meat.

PIG IN THE MIDDLE

Pig (or Piggy) in the Middle is the English, western Canadian and Australian name of a game that involves three people: a thrower of a ball, a catcher of the ball at some distance away, and in between them the piggy in the middle who has to try to intercept the ball as it is thrown from thrower to catcher. Elsewhere in the world the game is primarily known as Monkey in the Middle (eastern Canada, some parts of the USA and the Netherlands) or Keep Away (the rest of the USA). However, in Poland it is called Silly Johnny, in Denmark Butter Blob and in Turkey it is known as Rat in the Middle. In the USA, baseball terminology has additionally turned Piggy in the Middle into Pickle in the Middle to describe the situation when a runner is caught between bases.

THE INDISPENSABLE PIG

"Let us bow before the truly versatile genius of our porcine friends, and acknowledge, in all fairness, that they are as useful to us alive as dead. Without them, truffles might remain hidden in the earth, fodder for spiders and maggots instead of illustrious gourmands."

GRIMOD DE LA REYNIÈRE (1758-1837), *founder of a French gastronomic society*

THE DEPTH OF BOARDOM

A Japanese proverb states that, "A pig is wide of face but narrow in the back." But this is not intended just as a slightly surprising yet reasonably accurate description of the farmyard animal. It refers additionally to a suggested attribute of those born in the Year of the Pig – or in Japanese, the Year of the Boar (*inoshishi-doshi*). A person born in the Year of the Boar may thus be "wide of face but narrow in the back" – that is, may be one who has the air and outward appearance of someone who knows everything about everything, but who in fact has no more than a superficial knowledge of important matters with which to maintain such an illusion.

SKIN SPRAY & DEODORANTS

Manufacturers for the pig-farming industry have in recent decades begun to produce and advertise products aimed more at those who keep pigs as household pets. It began perhaps in the mid-1980s when the fad for keeping pot-bellied pigs took hold, and peaked again at the start of the new millennium when micro pigs became fashionable. Among the products currently advertised in this way are porcine skin sprays and deodorants. Skin sprays come mostly in spray bottles (not aerosol cans) and are promoted as water-based and containing only natural organic constituents, for daily use in eliminating fleas, ticks, lice and other external parasites. Deodorants more commonly take the form of food supplements to be added to the pig's ordinary daily diet, and are intended mainly to be effective at absorbing and neutralising the odours in the pig's excreted waste. Plant extracts in the supplements encourage rapid bacterial breakdown of the waste products, simultaneously reducing the amount of gases (particularly ammonia) released into the air.

PIGS IN MANHATTAN

Wall Street, New York, usa, was named after a wall that once ran along the northern edge of what is now Lower Manhattan. The wall was built by grain farmers who had been infuriated at the incursion of free-roaming pigs

into their valuable grain fields. The street then followed the length of the wall, and continued to be so called long after the disappearance of the pigs, the grain fields and the wall itself.

———————————— THE PIG-NOSED TURTLE ————————————

There is only one genus and species of pig-nosed turtle (*Carettochelys insculpta*, also known as the Fly River turtle or pitted-shell turtle), and it lives mainly in the rivers and lakes of southern New Guinea and northern Australia. It is much like many other turtles, but it does have a surprisingly pig-like double-nostrilled snout for a nose and rather bulbous eyes which add to the piggy effect. The females are on average heavier than the males – although females and males are generally the same overall size – and have a slightly humped carapace. The turtles emerge from water only to lay eggs in a nest made from scooped-out excavations onshore. As cold-blooded reptiles they are known to enjoy lying on top of underwater thermal vents for night-time warmth. Pig-nosed turtles are listed as "vulnerable" on the International Union for Conservation of Nature list of threatened species (known as the IUCN Red List), partly because they have long formed part of the standard diet of indigenous peoples.

———————————— BEAUTY IN THE BEAST ————————————

Portrait of a Pig is the title of a fairly well-known painting by the famous contemporary US artist James ("Jamie") Wyeth (born July 1946). The son, grandson and nephew of distinguished artists, Wyeth grew up within a socially prominent family, friends both with other artists (such as Andy Warhol) and with important political figures (such as members of the Kennedy clan). It was thus with apparently total seriousness that in 1970 on completing the *Portrait of a Pig* – in which the featured pig was a sow named Dun-Dun – Wyeth professed to have become "completely enamoured of her" mostly because "her eyes are so human, too – like a Kennedy's".

———————————— PIGS, EAGLES, FOXES & SKUNKS ————————————

The introduction of pigs allowed to roam wild on Santa Cruz Island, off the Californian coast of the USA, has had a dramatic effect on some of the animal and bird species indigenous to the region. Golden eagles, for example – hitherto restricted to preying on the occasional fox having flown in from the mainland – have found a new and abundant source of food, and have not only taken to preying on the wild pigs but have consequently taken up residence on the island themselves. The numbers of pigs on the island is currently sufficient to withstand the losses sustained to the eagles, but the number of foxes there has meanwhile swiftly declined and is expected to fall to zero very soon. In the absence of the foxes, however, the island's population of spotted skunks has increased – although their numbers too are likely to be kept in check to some extent by the golden eagles. All caused by the introduction of the pigs.

FOOD FOR THOUGHT

The number of pigs slaughtered in EU countries in 2008 totalled 255.107 million, divided as follows between the 27 states:

Country	Slaughtered (000s)	Country	Slaughtered (000s)	Country	Slaughtered (000s)
Austria	5,553	Germany	54,848	Malta	102
Belgium	11,157	Greece	1,913	Poland	22,321
Bulgaria	993	Holland	14,505	Portugal	5,976
Cyprus	725	Hungary	4,994	Romania	5,660
Czech Republic	3,804	Irish Republic	2,578	Slovakia	1,084
Denmark	20,790	Italy	13,616	Slovenia	381
Estonia	496	Latvia	524	Spain	41,306
Finland	2,459	Lithuania	937	Sweden	3,073
France	25,735	Luxembourg	150	UK	9,427

The number of pigs slaughtered in Australia in 2008 was 4.842 million, and in Canada was 21.520 million. The number of pigs slaughtered in the USA in the same year was 116.5 million, representing an average slaughter of 319,178 per working day. (This might be compared with the fact that, according to official figures, in the USA in 2008 nearly 25 million chickens were slaughtered every day.) It is China, however, that slaughters by far the most pigs, in 2008 alone accounting for at least 650 million.

THE POT-BELLIED PIG

POT-BELLIED PIGS are generally smaller than European or US farm pigs although their bodies are denser. Their bellies do indeed tend to bend and hang beneath them close to the ground. They have thick neck jowls and a short, stubby snout under beetling brows and pricked ears. And there is a slight dip or sway in the middle of the back towards a straightish tail. Once thought to be native only to Vietnam, some of the 14 subspecies of these pigs are now known to live also up in the mountains of Thailand more than 320 kilometres (200 miles) away. In both countries, however, purebred examples are becoming rarer – despite attempts at conservation – as breeds of larger pigs have been locally introduced (particularly in Vietnam, with European assistance) in order to improve overall pork production. Keeping a pot-bellied pig as a household pet became fashionable among the rich and famous of Europe and North America (such as actor George Clooney) during the mid-1980s.

KING NEPTUNE

KING NEPTUNE (originally named Parker Neptune) was a US Navy mascot pig used by an Illinois-based navy recruiter to raise $19 million in war bonds as a contribution towards the construction of the battleship *Illinois* between the years 1942 and 1946. Together with the recruiter Don C. Lingle, and an auctioneer, L. Oard Sitter, Neptune travelled to and fro across the state being put up for auction at major cities and social centres. For the first couple of years, the auctions were for the whole pig. After then, individual parts and attributes of Neptune were auctioned separately – his squeal fetched the magnificent sum of $25 more than once, although there was a remarkable occasion on which a single bristle of his went for $500. At the end of each event, the moneys (or promissory notes) were collected, and the pig – a Hereford red and white, customarily dressed in a blue naval blanket and wearing a crown and silver earrings – was in its entirety ceded back into the possession of the recruiter and the auctioneer to go on to the next auction. In 1946 King Neptune finally went into retirement to live on a farm just outside Anna, southern Illinois, where he died of pneumonia just two days before his eighth birthday in May 1950. He was buried with full military ceremony, and by order of the state authorities a tombstone was set up nearby on which the legend in part declared that the pig had raised $19 million "to help make a free world".

PIG, THE CARD GAME

This card game requires a pack/deck comprising only four cards of identical rank per player. (So if there were five players, all that would be needed would be 20 cards made up of five identical cards of each of the four suits – the four 4s, the four 5s, the four 6s, the four 7s and the four 8s, say) The object of the game is for a player to collect all four of one card. The reduced pack is shuffled before being dealt out so that each player receives four cards. Then, at a signal, each player passes on one card to the left while receiving simultaneously one card from the right. The signal is repeated, and these exchanges are made, until sooner or later someone will have four cards that are of identical value. However, instead of springing to his or her feet howling with uncontrollable joy, this player should as stealthily as possible do no more than touch a finger to the end of his or her nose ("the snout") and keep it there. Other players should then, as rapidly as they notice this gesture, do the same. The last to do so – depending on the rules agreed by players before beginning – is either the loser, and is eliminated (and the pack is further reduced by four cards for the next round), or loses one "life" of three (represented by the letters P-I-G). There can be no outright winner of this game: the last remaining two players are co-winners.

———————————— SPAM ————————————

Spam – correctly, SPAM™, in capitals (said originally to be a verbal contraction of "spiced ham") – is a canned, cooked pork product made either by or under licence from the Hormel Foods Corporation of Austin, Minnesota, USA. Its ingredients according to the label of the best-known (classic) variety are: chopped pork shoulder, ham meat, salt, water, modified potato starch (which acts as a binder) and sodium nitrite (which retains the colour). The jelly in Spam – more technically described as the gelatinous glaze or aspic – is formed as the meat stock cools. The main headquarters of Hormel Foods in Austin, Minnesota, with another base in Fremont, Nebraska, together produce Spam for the Americas and for Australasia. For Europe, Spam is produced under licence by Tulip in Denmark. And for Asia, Spam is produced under licence also in South Korea and the Philippines. Sales of Spam worldwide since its first appearance are now approaching 8 billion cans. At least five varieties with additional flavourings are manufactured, but are generally available only to suit regional tastes.

It was the *Monty Python* sketch first shown on TV in December 1970 parodying the countless ways in which Spam might be used as the centrepiece of a quickish meal – to the growing exasperation of a restaurant customer – that gave rise to the term "spam" (strictly in lower-case letters) to refer to unsolicited electronic mail. The sketch itself commemorates the fact that imported Spam was one of the few meat products not subject to rationing in the UK during and for some years after World War II, with the result that it inevitably formed a large and, in different guises, memorably repetitive part of the diet of much of the population.

———————————— HAIR OF THE HOG ————————————

Pig hair is the basis for a large number of household products, especially brushes of all kinds and uses. But there is inevitably hair left over from the manufacture of such products, and scientists in Japan have been trying to find out whether there is any practical and beneficial way in which it might be used or otherwise disposed of. Ultimately, the scientists' experiments came down to trying to find out a) whether the unwanted hair should simply be completely dissolved away somehow, or b) whether, if such dissolution is inevitably incomplete, the residue could be processed into some functionally valuable form. Pig hair – like human hair – is predominantly keratin (also the substance of human nails, bird claws and most animal hoofs). It seems that total dissolution is certainly possible in strong acids, but that in weak preparations of (alkaline) sodium hydroxide (NaOH) at a temperature of 70°C (158°F) maintained for some time, a residue is left that when spray-dried yields no fewer than nine of the so-called essential amino acids.

VARIABILITY IN THE PIG SKELETON

An adult pig's skeleton averages out at a basic 216 bones, compared with the adult human's 206. As in all mammals, the spine is the main axis of the skeleton, made up of vertebrae surrounding and protecting the spinal cord. In humans, the 33 vertebrae may be considered to comprise (from top to, er, bottom) seven cervical vertebrae, 12 thoracic vertebrae, five lumbar vertebrae, five fused sacral vertebrae, and between three and five (thus averaged at four) fused coccygeal vertebrae (the tailbone). Pigs, however, may have anything between 47 and 68 vertebrae, to a great extent depending on the breed – whether, for example, the pig has been bred for overall length (a greater number of vertebrae, with more ribs attached) or stocky solidity (a lesser number of vertebrae, with fewer but very slightly thicker ribs). Perhaps surprisingly, in view of the comparative shortness of the pig's tail, it is the tail which has by far the highest complement of structural bones: there are generally between 20 and 23 bones compared to the mere four coccygeal vertebrae in a human.

BLIND PIG MUSIC

FROM ITS BEGINNING in 1977 as a small blues club in a basement in Ann Arbor, Michigan, USA, founded by Blind Pig Café-owner Jerry Del Giudice and his friend Ed(ward) Chmelewski, Blind Pig Records has grown into one of the premier blues recording companies in the world. A number of top artists have performed blues, roots rock, zydeco, R&B and soul gospel on the Blind Pig label at one time or another. The company is currently based in San Francisco.

A "blind pig" was a speak-easy (a place where alcoholic drinks could be bought, and entertainment might be laid on too) during the 1920s–1930s US Prohibition era.

FOOD SUPPLEMENTS FOR STRESS

In a situation where a pig is likely to undergo stress – perhaps by being moved around outdoors, or by being introduced indoors as the household pet – it is sometimes helpful beforehand to administer vitamin E and/or selenium supplements as a dressing on top of the pig's usual food. Such supplements are commercially available, some of them even flavoured for sweetness, although care must be taken to adhere strictly to the dosages advised according to the type and weight of pig.

THE BARBECUE

It is a pleasantly fictitious piece of folk etymology that the word *barbecue* (illiterately and all too often in English spelled "barbeque") is derived from an expression used by French-speaking pirates in the Caribbean who loved to roast a pig on a spit, which they could then eat *de barbe à queue* "from beard to tail", because the entire pig was edible. The word is, however, derived not from French but (via Spanish) from the Caribbean language Taino, in which *barbacoa* refers to the raised platform or dais on which a whole animal – perhaps a pig, or instead an ox, sheep or goat – might be roasted above a fire, and around which the local inhabitants might stand to observe the cooking of what they would be hoping in due course to consume.

PIGLING BLAND

The Tale of Pigling Bland is a book for children written and illustrated by the English authoress Beatrix Potter (1866–1943). It is the story of a young pig obliged to leave home and find his own way to happiness. Pigling Bland, having been brought up by the sow Aunt Pettitoes but having with his seven siblings become too troublesome to manage, is thus shown the door. On his way to the local market to find work, he is delayed by getting lost in some woods but as darkness falls he manages to make room for himself in a farmer's chicken coop for the night. The farmer discovers him there in the morning and urges him to come and stay in his house – although the young pig is wary of such unexpected hospitality. There is, however, another pig staying in the house: a beautiful black Berkshire sow called Pig-wig. She has been stolen from her previous owner and fears now that the farmer whose house they are in means to turn her into ham and bacon. She wants to run away – and Pigling Bland quickly decides that they must both do so, and as soon as possible. They escape together at dawn the next day and, after having to evade at least one attempt to recapture them, make their way over the county boundary and a lot further still, until at last they feel safe enough to dance in their freedom together. The story was written from 1909 and published in 1913 – years in which Potter herself was likewise discovering a similar soul mate in local Lancashire solicitor William Heelis.

VOCAL HERITAGE

'Young pigs grunt as old pigs have grunted before them.'
Danish proverb

FOOT-&-MOUTH DISEASE

MANY PEOPLE are unaware that cattle and sheep are by no means the only farm animals able to contract this highly contagious viral disease. All cloven-footed animals can get it, and indeed the epidemic of 2001 in the UK that led to the culling of around 7 million sheep and cattle in five months and that cost the country an estimated £8 billion ($16 billion) is now thought to have been caused when sheep and cattle on one large farm came into contact with pigs on the same farm which had been fed food scraps that had been illegally imported and that contained infected meat. There are seven serotypes of the virus involved, all of which are extremely variable, which means that any attempt at prior vaccination relies on highly accurate diagnosis as to which variant of serotype is responsible for the danger. This is partly why quarantine and culling are so important in epidemic situations. In addition, the virus can be spread by physical contact with any other animal, including cats and dogs, rats and mice, and humans and their clothing. Major symptoms are open blisters in and around the mouth and bleeding ulcers on the legs and feet.

IS TASTE IMPORTANT TO PIGS?

Pigs have the capacity to taste things twice as sensitively as humans do. But is taste important to them? In some respects it is, for like cats (which have a sense of taste that is only about 3% of the human sense of taste) but unlike dogs (17% of the human sense of taste), pigs avoid foods that have made them sick after their first consumption, and it is apparently a memory of the taste that deters them from repeating the experience. Yet overall, it has to be said that taste seems not to be as important to pigs as the sheer fact of eating and of feeling comfortably full as often and as long as possible. This is after all why pigs have a reputation for being gluttonous (hence such expressions as "to pig out", "to make a pig of oneself") and why they really do gorge themselves at every opportunity.

THE WHEEL OF REBIRTH

IN BUDDHIST ICONOGRAPHY the pig generally represents desire of all kinds. However, the ultimate aim of the Buddhist creed is to free oneself from all desires and so find release (*moksha*) from this world. The pig is therefore one of three animals often depicted at the hub of the Wheel of Rebirth (also called the Wheel of Life or *Bhavachakra*) representing the major earthly impediments to enlightenment: desire, hatred and delusion.

——— RUN YOUR HAND DOWN A PIG'S EAR ———

Cross section

The pig's ear handrail is usually intended as a secondary railing or bannister, rather than as something to grasp and, if necessary, pull on. For that reason, manufacturers advertise it as most suitable on staircases with solid vertical walls on both sides or on wide staircases where current building regulations demand more than just a bannister on the overhang side. The rail fixes directly onto a wall, and no brackets are required. The wood used is ordinarily a hardwood such as oak or ash, but rails made of softer woods (such as pine) are also readily available. It is described as a pig's ear handrail because someone at some time thought the cross-section faintly resembled the porcine appendage.

——— SCHWEINFURT, GERMANY ———

Schweinfurt is an industrial city in Bavaria, central Germany. Renowned for its iron and steel works and in former times also for the production of the highly toxic pigment Schweinfurt green, the city is now of mostly modern construction although it apparently began as a tiny eighth-century community at a location on the major River Main where pigs could easily be driven across the water – it was the "swine ford". Several bridges now span the river, which has long since been canalised. A few medieval buildings remain around the airy Motherwell Park (named after the town in Scotland with which Schweinfurt is twinned) and the central market square. The population in 2008 was officially 53,566.

——— PINKY & PERKY ———

PINKY AND PERKY are a couple of pigs that, as string puppets, featured on British children's TV in their own shows and series between the years 1957 and 1971. Created by Czechoslovakian immigrants Jan and Vlasta Dalibor, they sang (mostly cover versions of contemporary pop songs in high-pitched squeaky voices), they danced (jerkily) and they performed comedy sketches with such human foils as actor John Slater, TV announcer Roger Moffat, actor-writer Jimmy Thompson and ponderous comedian Fred Emney. Not well known outside the UK, Pinky and Perky nonetheless made no fewer than six appearances on the *Ed Sullivan Show* on US TV – on one occasion sharing the billing with The Beatles and Morecambe and Wise – and released 24 pop singles, 16 EPS (extended-play records) and 11 albums (LPS).

An all-new 52-episode CGI-animated series of *The Pinky and Perky Show* was recorded for BBC Television and began broadcasting in November 2008.

———— TO CURE HEATSTROKE IN A PIG ————

THE SIGNS OF HEATSTROKE in a pig can become visible in a remarkably short space of time. They include panting and laboured breathing with the mouth held wide open, a rapid pulse and a high temperature. The first thing to do is to try to cool the pig down. Fetch a trough or aluminium bath, fill it with cool water to a depth of about 5 centimetres (2 inches) and stand the pig in the water. Unless the pig is quite used to being hosed down, *do not pour water over the pig's head or body* or the pig may fear drowning and go into shock – cool the pig *only from the feet up*. If this treatment fails to evoke a positive response within three or four minutes, seek emergency assistance from a vet.

———————— SEEING SPOTS ————————

"Spots" is the modern (1960s) US term for what Americans otherwise call "spotted hogs" or "spotted swine" because they are predominantly white (that is, very light grey) with spots of much darker colour mostly on the neck and back. They are popular with US farmers because – as has been formally proved in the country's testing stations – they gain weight rapidly and they pass on this economically useful trait to their offspring.

However, the US Spots have very little in common (a minimal amount of cross-breeding in the first decades of the 20th century) with the traditional European (and specifically British) type of pig called the Spot, exemplified in particular by the renowned Gloucester Old Spot – now inevitably known in the USA as the Gloucester Old Spots.

Among the largest pigs in England, the Gloucester Old Spot is generally described as black and white, but the white areas are in fact greyish pink and the amount of black in the form of spots has over the last couple of decades been reduced by selective breeding to the extent that spots of any real size have become rare. The pigs have heavy, rounded, drooping ears, and are said to be excellent foragers and ground-grazers – which is not surprising since they were in former times partly reared on windfall apples and were sometimes alternatively called Orchard pigs. (Gloucestershire in southwestern England is a county still famous for producing traditional apples.) The sows give birth to large litters and have abundant milk. Such good qualities should perhaps have made the Spot more popular than it is.

——— THAI BUDDHISM & CHINESE ASTROLOGY ———

RURAL CULTURE in Thailand adopted the Chinese astrological zodiac in around the sixth century AD, when Buddhism was sweeping across the Asiatic nations from India to the east. As in Japan, the zodiac and its 12 animals (in which the twelfth is the pig or boar) remains strongly identified with the Buddhist religion and way of life in Thailand, to the extent that the 12 animals have over the centuries each become linked with one major Buddhist temple in the country. It is now the custom for as many people as possible to make a special pilgrimage at least once in their lifetime to the temple associated with the animal of their birth year. The temple associated with the zodiacal pig is Wat Phra That Doi Tung (initially constructed AD 911). It is in the northern province of Chiang Rai at an altitude of 1,800 metres (5,490 feet) up in the mountains (Doi Tung is the name of the individual summit) close to the Thai border with Myanmar (Burma). It is reached by a beautiful path lined each side with hanging bronze bells. In summer it becomes extremely crowded.

Elsewhere in northern Thailand, however, the Year of the Elephant has largely replaced the Year of the Pig for astrological purposes.

——————— HOG-ART-H ———————

William Hogarth (1697–1764), the famous English social portraitist and satirical printmaker, effectively invented the cartoon strip by producing sequences of engravings that told a story. Many of his works were on contemporary themes of moral interest – particularly notable were *A Harlot's Progress* (1731), *A Rake's Progress* (1735) and *Marriage à-la-mode* (1743–5) – which not only brought him considerable fame but on occasion also influenced the legislative authorities of the time to introduce new laws or to modify existing ones. In addition he was friends with many other artists and prominent actors, one of whom – the celebrated actor and theatrical producer David Garrick – wrote this epitaph on Hogarth's death:

> *Farewell, great Painter of Mankind*
> *Who reach'd the noblest point of Art,*
> *Whose pictur'd Morals charm the Mind*
> *And through the Eye correct the Heart.*

Yet Hogarth had been born of a poor London family (his father was a teacher of Latin in a local school) – though not so poor, perhaps, as to be consistent with the derivation of his surname: Old English *hogg hierde* "swine-herd".

———————— FERAL PIGS IN AUSTRALIA ————————

Towards the end of 2008 it was reported in Australia that:

✳ feral pigs were present in around 40% of the entire land area of the country
✳ the total number of feral pigs was in excess of 24 million
✳ feral pigs tend to live and forage in groups that may consist of 60 animals or more
✳ feral pig group numbers may increase annually by more than 100% in good conditions depending on the availability of food
✳ a feral sow averages 5 piglets per litter and can give birth twice a year
✳ the very numbers of feral pigs, and the fact that they live in large groups, constitutes a threat to many indigenous Australian animal and reptile species
✳ in some sheep-farming areas of Australia, feral pigs regularly kill up to 40% of the lambs per season
✳ feral pigs are also carriers of diseases that are dangerous – sometimes fatal – both to other animals and to humans (notably leptospirosis in Queensland)
✳ other damage caused by feral pigs includes soil erosion and land degradation – sometimes endangering the continued existence of entire plant species – the fouling and poisoning of water supplies and the destruction of essential fencing
✳ the trapping and killing of feral pigs is regarded as a necessity in many areas of Australia, and the meat from the culled animals – after due inspection – may be sold (chiefly for export).

———— CANCER TREATMENT USING PIGS' BLOOD ————

P IGS' BLOOD CONTAINS an unusual quantity of the light-sensitive substances called porphyrins (which is at least partly why pigs suffer so much from sunburn). Porphyrins bind to lipoproteins, which contribute to making up the membrane that encloses every body cell. Cancer cells form membranes faster than normal body cells do – and so accumulate more porphyrins. Now scientists have combined certain of the porphyrins found in pigs' blood to form a synthetic porphyrin they call Photofrin®, which absorbs energy from light at specific wavelengths and in a related chemical reaction releases oxygen. If a human cancer patient is injected with Photofrin, it accumulates with other porphyrins in the cancerous tissue as part of the cancerous cell membranes. When a laser beam of the specific wavelength is then introduced to the cancerous area, the Photofrin absorbs the energy and goes on to release oxygen, which damages the cell membranes and destroys most of the cell contents – thus eliminating the cancer cells. The laser beam has to be focused precisely on the cancerous tissue, but nearby healthy tissue should remain entirely unaffected. The only side effect is that for about a month until the Photofrin wears off inside the body, the patient must be kept out of direct sunlight or is likely to suffer from painful sunburn.

THE SPEEDY PIG

An unconfirmed report claims that on 29 April 1984 in Hamburg, Germany, a pig named Kloten-Joe II ran 100 metres (109 yards) in 11 seconds. That would equate to an average speed of 32.73 kilometres/hour (20.45 miles per hour). Much more recently, the US Fish and Wildlife Service has published a list of the greatest speeds achieved by different animals. The cheetah, at 112 kilometres/hour (70 miles per hour), is obviously at the top of the list. Beneath, the pig is a rather lowly 31st, at 17.6 kilometres/hour (11 miles per hour), between the squirrel (19.2 kilometres/hour (12 miles per hour)) and the chicken (14.4 kilometres/hour (9 miles per hour)). Perhaps it might be of some comfort to the pig to know that its wild African relative the warthog is as high as 22nd on the list at 48 kilometres/hour (30 miles per hour)), apparently equal with the white-tailed deer, the grizzly bear and the domestic cat.

PIGS IN CLOVER, THE GAME

PIGS IN CLOVER is the Victorian English name for a game that developed into, first, a hand-held tray on which a marble or silver ball was tilted into one or more sockets, and so scored points or completed a course, and second, a more complicated three-dimensional course in which a ball was manoeuvred by using two dials to tilt a tray (in two dimensions each) so that the ball avoided either holes or pins to complete the highly convoluted course. The original game, however, involved a tray of sockets into which quite a number of marbles might somewhat haphazardly be rolled by tilting the tray, scoring a total of points corresponding to the sum of the numbers marked against filled sockets. The name is derived from the notion of a pig's settling its snout comfortably – and profitably – into a hole it has dug for itself in the ground.

THE EMPRESS OF BLANDINGS

The Empress of Blandings is a prize pig that features in the stories of P. G. Wodehouse about the eccentric Lord Emsworth who lives in Blandings Castle. She is an enormous black Berkshire sow who regularly wins trophies in the Fat Pigs class at the local Shropshire Agricultural Show – to the fury of Lord Emsworth's neighbour and rival pig-owner Sir Gregory Parsloe-Parsloe. In the stories, the Empress is often kidnapped or otherwise imperilled, and has to be rescued. It is interesting how many echoes there are in these basic details of the Empress of Blandings that are reminiscent of Beatrix Potter's children's story involving Pigling Bland. The names Blandings and Pigling Bland are an obvious example. Pigling Bland's lady-love was also a Berkshire sow, and had been stolen from her owner.

———————— THE FABLE OF THE PIG & THE OWL ————————

It was twilight, and a pig – relaxing in the warm air at the doorway to his shelter in the farm's outer field – was conversing with an owl perched on the point of the arch over the triangular doorway. "So tell me, owl," said the pig, "why do the humans think you are a wise old bird, eh?" The owl blinked heavily a couple of times, and shrugged as much as anyone can shrug who has no shoulders. "I'm not too sure," he said, "but it may be because I'm good at what I do, and I can see things from a long way away. I don't get too close to the humans, and I am free to get on with my life and look forward to the future. But what about you, pig? You are said to be clever too." The pig in turn shrugged as much as anyone can shrug whose neck is so massive as to overlap the shoulders. "Oh yes, I suppose I have a bit of knowledge, and I can make use of it better than some," he said. "I don't mind getting close to humans, for they make sure that I have shelter and I get as much as I want to eat and drink, even if it means I'm not free to wander around and find my own food as you have to do. Yet I wouldn't say that the little knowledge I have actually makes me *wise*, though." The owl stretched his neck and peered into the gathering darkness. "But do you look forward to the future?" he asked. The pig slowly shook his large head. "I don't think about it," he said. "I've got better things to think about, and I just live one day at a time." There was silence for a few minutes, during which it occurred forcefully to the owl that it may take knowledge to be wise, but it takes wisdom not to seek too much knowledge.

———————————— THE PIGFISH ————————————

THE PIGFISH is a term applied to a number of different species of fish, but distinguishing between the fish involved is complicated because some of them are known alternatively in English as hogfish, and there are also porkfish. Pigfish is, for example, a name for fishes of the family Congiopodidae (also called horsefishes and racehorses), but also more specifically for *Orthopristis chrysoptera* (also called the redmouth grunt, hogfish, or sailor's choice), for *Orthopristis ruber* (also called the Corocoro grunt or spotted pigfish) and for *Bodianus unimaculatus* (also called the golden-spot hogfish). Meanwhile, in Swedish and Norwegian, *svinfisk* ("pig-fish") is the common name of *Anisotremus virginicus*, which in English is the Atlantic porkfish – closely related to the Panama porkfish, *Anisotremus taeniatus* – and the *röd* (red) *svinfisk* is the common name of *Decodon puellaris*, otherwise known in English as the red hogfish.

─────────── CHINESE SPICED PIG'S TONGUE ───────────

INGREDIENTS

a pig's tongue (fresh)
3–4 tablespoons light or dark soy sauce
½ teaspoon ginger sherry (sherry in which ginger has been steeped for some time)
1 teaspoon sugar
a pinch of salt
a dash of pepper
6 tablespoons of water

METHOD

1. Wash the tongue thoroughly, drain it, and put it by, temporarily, under cover.
2. Blend together all the other ingredients in a pan just large enough to fit the tongue inside, and bring them to the boil. This is to be the marinade.
3. Allow the marinade to cool completely.
4. Put the tongue in the marinade – which should cover it – in the pan. Bring the liquid to the boil, and let it simmer for as long as it takes for the tongue to become tender.
5. Let it cool a little – but while the tongue is still hot, skin it.
6. Then allow it to cool completely.
7. On a cutting-board, slice the cold tongue as thinly as possible at an angle of 45 degrees to its horizontal length, from one end to the other.
8. Serve the slices arranged in one or more neat rows.

─────── THINGS THAT GO GREEN IN THE NIGHT ───────

In January 2006 a BBC News report described how scientists from the National University's Department of Animal Science and Technology in Taiwan had successfully bred three pigs which, when a blue light was shone on them in otherwise dark surroundings, emanated a bright yellow-green aura. Even in daylight the pigs' skin had a greenish tinge, and their eyes, teeth and feet were genuinely green. In fact, the scientists said that the pigs' internal organs – even their hearts – were green too. That was because they were transgenic pigs: genetic material from jellyfish had been added to them while they were still embryos. The purpose of this research was to add to the world's increasing knowledge of the nature and use of stem cells, with particular reference to the study of human diseases and other conditions that require the replacement of body tissues. If some stem cells from one of these pigs are injected into another animal, developments are easy to trace by means of scans rather than via invasive surgery because the pig's genetic material encodes a protein that shows up as green. It is hoped that in due course these pigs will mate with ordinary pigs – and will pass on their green credentials.

MIXING WITH OTHER PIGS

THE ADDITION OF A PIG to an already established group of pigs requires the new pig to locate its place in the hierarchy. This may take a day or two, and involve some skirmishes and combative threats, but once dominance is settled between any two individuals, encounters thereafter usually consist only of snappish grunts and menacing gestures. From an onlooker's viewpoint, the top pig in the hierarchy can be determined by spotting which pig tends to get its way by physically pushing others around. A submissive pig may gently rub the back or belly of a more dominant pig with its snout. Being top pig is a pretty secure position – the hierarchy once established is so stable that the top pig can be removed from the rest of the group for up to perhaps four weeks and, when reintroduced to the group again, still be top pig.

More serious forms of combat occur among groups that comprise solely uncastrated male pigs, often resulting in severe bites. Some adult boars become extremely aggressive and may have to be kept completely isolated.

WHERE ARE THE KNUCKLES ON A PIG?

It is quite common to find recipes that talk about "pigs' knuckles" but very difficult to find any literature or diagram that explains exactly what and where the knuckles are. After all, a pig doesn't have a fist or fingers (which is where humans have knuckles). What is worse, different culinary authorities tend to imply that the knuckles are different parts of the pig anyway. Some – especially in the USA – evidently reckon that the knuckles are the same as the "feet" or trotters. Others – particularly in the UK – suggest that knuckles are the pig's hocks (upper forelimbs) or legs (upper hindlimbs) chopped in slices. And yet others – but far fewer of them – would have you believe that they are the pig's equivalents of the knee, ankle, elbow and wrist joints with surrounding flesh. But why should any of these be described as knuckles?

PIG IN THE PARLOUR

We Have a Pig in the Parlour is an old song, seemingly Irish in origin, sung to the tune of what is now much better known as *For He's a Jolly Good Fellow*. It is meant to accompany a relatively simple – i.e. potentially tediously repetitive – dance in which couples form a circle and with linked hands step daintily around a solitary person in the middle (who is the pig in the parlour) for a chorus and a verse of the song, after which the solitary person is allowed to break into the circle and replace one member of it. That member then becomes the pig in the parlour, at which point the first line of the chorus becomes *We have a NEW pig in the parlour*.

—————— WEIGHT ON A PIG-FARMER'S MIND ——————

IN ENGLISH, as in many other languages, young pigs may be described by pig-farmers using a number of terms according to each pig's weight. Thus a "feeder pig" is a piglet that weighs only between 18 and 23 kilograms (40 and 50 pounds), "growing pigs" are those that weigh between 18 and 57 kilograms (40 and 125 pounds) and "finishing pigs" weigh between 57 kilograms (125 pounds) and "market weight" – around 104 kilograms (230 pounds) at which they may instead be described as "hogs". Healthy young pigs gain from 680 to 800 grams (1½ to 1¾ pounds) per day, if fed properly – a rate that may be taken into account when timing the marketing of a "finished" pig or hog.

FEEDER PIG
18–23 kg (40–50 lbs)

GROWING PIG
18–57 kg (40–125 lbs)

FINISHING PIG
57–104 kg (125–230 lbs)

—————— THE ORKNEY & FAROE ISLANDS ——————

The Orkney islands just off the northern coast of Scotland are named after the wild boars that roamed on them when the Norwegian Vikings occupied the area in the ninth century AD. The dialectal Norse *orc* meant "boar" (cognate with Latin *porcus*), and the islands thus became the *Orcen-øyar* "boar islands". However, the word *orc* thereafter came to be used of the seals that abound in the waters around those islands – which is why they are just as often described today as the "seal islands". Much further north still, about halfway between Iceland and Norway, lie the Faroe islands. These too are said to have been named by Norse Vikings, although this time possibly after the sheep there, as reputedly introduced by the seafaring St Brendan on one of his celebrated voyages in the sixth century. The

modern Danish and Swedish for "sheep" is *får* and modern Norwegian *fårekjøtt* means "mutton". Yet these Scandinavian words for "sheep" would seem to be dialectal variants of an underlying Germanic term originally meaning "pig" – the cognate Anglo-Saxon *fōr* or *fearh* meant "piglet" or "litter of piglets" (again also cognate with Latin *porcus*), from which modern English has derived *farrow*.

―――――――――――― HOG CHOLERA ――――――――――――

HOG CHOLERA is the former name of what is now more technically known as classical swine fever (CSF) – but "hog cholera" gives a much better initial idea of how contagious and dangerous the disease is, especially to those who might confuse "classical swine fever" with swine flu. The CSF virus generally causes death in pigs, after violent and painful symptoms, within two weeks. There is no treatment, let alone cure, and affected animals have to be culled together with their groups. Some forms of vaccination are possible to try to prevent the disease from spreading to nearby unaffected groups. Humans appear to be immune to the disease but may, if careless, carry the virus on their clothing.

――――――― THE STORY OF MAC DA THO'S PIG ―――――――

This episode from Celtic mythology (in Irish called *Scéla mucce Meic Da Tho*) despite its very clear title is in fact more about a hound than it is about a pig. Mac Da Tho was King of Leinster in Ireland sometime in early Irish history, and was the owner of the said hound, named Ailbe, which, because of its exceptional qualities, was coveted by the royal families of several neighbouring kingdoms. Mac Da Tho made the mistake of trying to appease two of the more bellicose ones – Ulster and Connaught – by promising them both that he would give the hound to them. Unhappily for everyone concerned, the royal offspring of the two kingdoms arrived simultaneously with attendant warriors to collect the dog. Under the laws of contemporary hospitality, Mac Da Tho was obliged to hold a great feast at which the main dish was a gigantic boar, served with great ceremony involving the strict observance of a hierarchy relating to royal status and to battle honours in warfare to date. The party with the best claim to royal status and with an unmatched battle record could expect to be accorded the finest and most prestigious cut of the boar's meat. Mac Da Tho suggested that whoever could make such a claim and prove it should also take the hound – a suggestion that he might have hoped would let him off the hook. But the champions of Ulster and Connaught would hear of nobody but themselves as those of obvious supremacy, and were vociferous in proclaiming their battle honours – particularly in warfare against each other – in order to assert their precedence and take the dog. The boar was forgotten (other than in the title of the story later). Taunts and counter-taunts flew between the two. It was then proposed that the hound itself be encouraged to choose between the parties. The champions sullenly agreed, still seething. The dog, once released, for one reason or another then wandered towards the champion of Ulster, who managed to grab it, but even as he tried to hustle the animal away on his chariot, the chariot of the opposing Connaught prince rammed it, and its main shaft went straight through the dog, transfixing it. Outright war between Ulster and Connaught broke out once again.

THE CELESTIAL SOW

Originally goddess only of the night sky and protectress of the stars, the ancient Egyptian deity Nut (whose name might well be cognate with the English word *night*) in time became goddess of the sky in general, and was frequently depicted arched on her fingers and toes above the earth god Geb, the space between them filled by Shu, god of the air. But the stars still formed the main part of Nut's body – and in that context, Nut might also be depicted as the Celestial Sow suckling the multitude of piglets that were the stars. At the coming of the

dawn Nut swallowed her entire litter as she simultaneously gave birth to Ra, the sun god. And as dusk fell each evening, Nut swallowed Ra as she simultaneously gave birth again to her piglet stars. This is the cycle of birth, death and rebirth as the Egyptians knew it, represented even more forcefully in the story of Nut's son Osiris as resurrected by his wife, Nut's daughter Isis.

WIBBLY PIG

The series of picture books that feature Wibbly Pig – and his favourite toys, Pigley, Flop and Dimple – are written and illustrated by Mike Inkpen. They are intended for very young children and infants, and so are produced as "board books" with thick-card glossy pages that are easy both for young fingers to turn over and for parents to clean. Most of the books have been translated into numerous languages and are thus popular worldwide. A British TV series based on the books was first shown in 2009.

GOING THE WHOLE HOG

To "go the whole hog" is an English expression meaning to do something thoroughly and completely when there is the option not to. It may be derived from a time when a "hog" was a slang term in Britain for the 12 pence coin known as a shilling (later to become slang in the USA for a dime or for any foreign coin of unknown value), and so to "go the whole hog" might be to lash out all of 12 pence on a round of drinks in an alehouse. A rather more obvious derivation – commonly cited with reference either to the English poet William Cowper's poem *Hypocrisy Detected* (1779) or to the followers of US presidential candidate Andrew Jackson (1828) – concerns the roasting and eating of a whole hog rather than of merely specific cuts and portions.

———————————— PIETRAINS ————————————

The Pietrain breed of pig – which originated in the village of Piétrain in the Jordoigne municipality in Wallonia, Belgium, and should therefore be pronounced in the French fashion – is of medium size but stocky and sturdy and wide in the back and hams. It is ordinarily described as white with black spots and blotches although the "white" is actually light pink and the "black" is a rather dingy grey that makes the pig look almost as if it has gone slightly mouldy in places. Unusually for a pig, the ears are carried erect. The breed is known for an exceptionally high ratio of lean meat to fat, which makes it useful for fresh meat processing. Most pork is sold as fresh meat in Belgium – and by 2007 Pietrain pigs constituted one-quarter of all pigs in that country.

———————————— SCROFULOUSNESS ————————————

"SCROFULA" is in English (with cognate variants in French, German and many other languages) a slightly old-fashioned term for what was once a fairly common disease in humans: tuberculosis of the lymph glands, particularly the lymph glands in the neck – a condition described technically as cervical tuberculous lymphadenopathy. From the Middle Ages until at least the 18th century in Europe, the condition was alternatively called "the king's evil" because it was firmly believed that it could be cured by the touch of a reigning monarch. Indeed, King Henry IV of France (ruled 1589–1610) held sessions for up to 1,500 sufferers at a time to be touched and healed, and the 1633 *Book of Common Prayer* of the Anglican Church contained a specific liturgical rite by which the ceremony might be performed in the Chapel Royal or elsewhere. The word "scrofula", however, goes back much further. It is the Latin diminutive of *scrofa* "a breeding sow" (as in the current scientific term for the wild boar, *Sus scrofa*). Evidently the large, rounded lumps under the skin around the neck of a scrofulous patient looked like little sows growing and breeding there.

As monarchs not unreasonably began to be less willing to touch diseased patients – George I of Great Britain (ruled 1714–1727) simply refused to do it – to be "scrofulous" gradually took on the meaning of merely looking diseased or mangy, and it may be that the current word *scruffy* is no more than a modern contraction of the term.

A MATTER OF PRESENTATION

'You can put lipstick on a hog – it's still a pig.'

ANN RICHARDS, *US TV political commentator, on attempts by political leaders to enhance the voter appeal of their own candidates in a forthcoming election*

THE SOW OF MUSIC

Many nursing sows croon gently to their piglets at feeding time.

EZILI DANTOR & THE CREOLE PIG

IN HAITIAN VOODOO, Ezili Dantor (alternatively spelled Erzulie Danthor) is the *lwa* or patron spirit of motherhood, especially single motherhood, and associated particularly with the colours gold and blue and, until the 1980s, with the Creole pig. This was a very hardy type of pig well suited to the rigours and privations of rural life among the peasants of Haiti. In the 1980s, however, the Haitian government under strong pressure from the USA culled all the Creole pigs in the country because they were said (by US biologists) either to have contracted or to be in danger of contracting African swine fever. Replacement pigs were brought in from the USA but were soon found both to be unable to cope with the standard way of life in Haiti and to be far too expensive in upkeep. Since 1990, Haitian and French agronomists have therefore bred a new variety of pig that has most of the required physical characteristics of the old Creole pigs, and a second replacement programme is currently under way. If it is as successful as hoped, the new Creole pig will no doubt take the place of the old as one of the favoured customary sacrifices to Ezili Dantor.

THE VALUE OF REFLECTION

According to the supposed folklore of certain parts of Europe, pigs become terrified if they see their reflection in a mirror. This is, however, quite untrue. Biologists at Cambridge University in England in late 2009 carried out an experiment in which eight pigs, in pairs, were introduced to a large mirror at ground level, and encouraged to familiarise themselves with its properties for five hours. None was terrified; only one became aggressive and charged at its own reflection in the mirror. The others all studied it at close quarters and then from various angles. After this familiarisation, each pig was individually placed in a pen with an angled mirror and a partition, behind which lay some treats such as chunks of apple. Seven of the eight pigs immediately looked behind the partition and found the treats. A control group of pigs which had never seen a mirror before just looked for the treats behind the mirror.

THE BABIROUSA

Babirousas are members of the pig family Suidae but not members of the *Sus* genus to which boars and pigs belong. Instead, they constitute four species of the genus *Babyrousa*: the hairy or golden babirousa (B. *babyrussa*), the Bola Batu babirousa (B. *bolabatuensis*), the (North) Sulawesi babirousa (B. *celebensis*) and the Togian babirousa (B. *togeanensis*). Only the Sulawesi babirousa has been studied in any scientific detail, and indeed, much of the lifestyle and behavioural traits of the other babirousas remain largely unknown. Babirousas live only on certain islands of Indonesia. The name is derived from Indonesian *babi rusa* "pig deer", and this literal translation is occasionally used for them in English too, although they look more like domestic pigs with long, thin legs and enormously elongated tusks than they do deer. Their preferred habitat is tropical forest, in which they forage mainly for fruit. Although a protected species, babirousas are listed as "vulnerable" by the International Union for Conservation of Nature (IUCN) chiefly because babirousa meat is still considered a traditional delicacy by local hunters.

THE GOOD LUCK PIG

In Germany, the pig has traditionally been a symbol of good fortune. In fact, the German expression *Ich habe Schwein gehabt* ("I have had pork") actually means "I've had a stroke of luck." The symbol is particularly associated with Christmastime. From the late 19th century to the first decades of the 20th, a "good luck pig" (*Glucksschwein*) commonly featured as the main design on Christmas cards and Christmas decorations, and even today a marzipan pig is a frequent little gift between friends during that season.

TURNING WATER INTO SWINE

One half to two-thirds of a pig's body is made up of water, depending on the proportions of lean muscle tissue (75% water) and fat (only 10% water). This is not far different from the overall amount of water in the average adult human body (males around 60%, females around 55%). Like humans – and in truth like most other mammals – pigs can live considerably longer without food than they can without water.

UNUSUAL CONDITIONS IN IRELAND

> "The world is quiet, and the pig is in the sty."
> *Irish proverb*

WHAT A BOAR

The fourth Labour of Hercules/Herakles, according to ancient Greek myth, was to capture alive the enormous boar that lived on Mount Erymanthus (in Arcadia, on the Peloponnese in southern Greece) and that seemed to take perverse pleasure in ravaging the countryside all around. One main problem for Hercules was that the boar could run faster than he could, especially uphill. But he managed, with some strategy, to chase it into a high valley and into a snowdrift there, which slowed the boar down considerably. He was then able to jump on the boar's rump and bind the animal with strong chains. So trussed, the animal was thereafter transported on Hercules' back to Mycenae.

THE RELIGIOUS BAN ON EATING PORK

THOSE PEOPLE who do not adhere to the Jewish or the Islamic religions are often unaware of how specifically the relevant scriptural texts forbid the consumption of pork and of various other meats. In Judaism, the Kashrut (the dietary laws decreeing what is acceptable; related adjective, *kosher*) in respect of pork rely mainly on the verse in the Torah that states:

> *And the swine, though he divide the hoof, and be cloven-footed,*
> *yet he cheweth not the cud; he is unclean to you. Of their flesh shall ye not eat,*
> *and their carcase shall ye not touch: they are unclean to you.*

In the Judaeo-Christian Bible (the Old Testament), these words appear as Leviticus 11: 7–8, and it is because they appear there that some more strictly literal-minded Christians likewise observe the ban.

The main text on the subject in the Koran (2: 173) refers back to the same prohibition (*haraam*) but adds a note of possible mitigation:

> *[God] has forbidden you carrion, blood and the flesh of swine, and indeed any flesh that*
> *is nominally consecrated to any other [deity] than Allah. But whoever is physically compelled*
> *to eat any of these remains sinless just so long as there is no question at all of personal*
> *wilfulness or deliberate religious disobedience. For Allah is compassionate, is merciful.*

---------------------- MICRO BENEFITS ----------------------

The fad in the first decade of the 21st century for keeping a micro pig as a household pet – as apparently enjoyed by some young, wealthy urbanites – seems now to be declining. The result is that breeders are endeavouring to appeal to a different market and are therefore putting forward new reasons for potential owners to buy the pigs. Micro pigs are thus now advertised as excellent companions for the elderly and for those who suffer from allergies to other household pets, particularly cats and their fur. However, although the pigs may be diminishing in size, their initial purchase price is evidently not doing so, and it would seem optimistic to expect such an expensive outlay to be made either by the elderly in general or by those who may have to defray continual medical expenses on treatment for their allergy.

---------------- SHOCK! HORROR! PIGS EAT GRASS ----------------

One day in 1976 when hunting in the Haurangi mountains of New Zealand, a young man called Ivan Churcher found a lost feral piglet. He took it home to the rural southern Wairarapa area, christened it Barry, and soon found that the pig was very quick to learn: he would come when called and sit on command. Moreover, Barry turned out to be a remarkably good companion, prepared to enjoy Ivan's rather less than respectable home lifestyle to the full. Not only did Barry like the odd bottle of beer – which he would pick up in his mouth and drain in one long swallow, before replacing the bottle on the ground – but he would chew contentedly on Ivan's cannabis leaves while the man smoked the weed in his pipe. The inevitable happened. In the early 1980s Ivan was arrested for the cultivation of cannabis plants and for the possession and use of the drug. In court he pleaded guilty on all charges – but claimed in mitigation that the plants were grown not only for his own use but also for Barry. Even the prosecuting counsel conceded that the pig was almost certainly an addict. Ivan was surprisingly but accordingly given a minimum sentence – 75 hours' community service – which made headlines in the local papers that were in turn syndicated to the national and then the international media. Barry became a celebrity, appearing in rural shows where people would for charity try to guess his weight or how many biscuits he could eat within a set time.

---------------------- MISS PIGGY ----------------------

Miss Piggy is one of the central characters of tv's *The Muppet Show*. Voiced by Frank Oz until 2002, Miss Piggy (who, when asked, once said that her forename was "Miss") became popular between the 1970s and 1990s, selling a vast selection of personalised merchandise (such as a perfume called *Moi*) and being the ostensible author of a bestselling book (*Miss Piggy's Guide to Life*, 1981).

PIGS DON'T WANT TO FLY

Because of their poor vision, and because when awake they tend by nature always to be foraging for more food, pigs generally rely on being able to see the ground immediately under their trotters. Few of them therefore have any head for heights. Young piglets squeal when they are picked up because they no longer have the reassurance of solid ground beneath them.

UP THE TROTTERS!

The players of the English Premiership soccer team Bolton Wanderers Football Club are known as "the Trotters" by their supporters because a former football ground (the one before Burnden Park, at which they played for 102 years until 1997) was located right next to a pig farm – so close that a shot which went over the top of the goal at one end used to land among the feet of the pigs, and the ball had (occasionally several times in one game) thus to be retrieved "from the trotters".

THE PIGTAIL DRAIN TUBE

A PIGTAIL TUBE is a type of catheter used to drain body fluids directly from inside the human body to the outside. Conditions in which this might be necessary include a blockage in the ureter (requiring drainage of urine from a kidney) or in the bile duct (requiring drainage of bile). The tube is inserted via a minor surgical procedure following x-ray scanning for precision in location. Some risk of haemorrhage or infection is inevitable, particularly where the tube enters and leaves the outer skin surface, although such risks should be minimised by hospital protocol. It is called a pigtail tube because it emerges from the body horizontally before curving down to its tip, just like a pig's tail.

GREASED PIG CHASE

Chasing one or more greased pigs is a form of sporting contest that is popular in many pig-farming areas of the world, but especially in the southern USA. It is often one of the events that take place at state and county fairs in the USA, and at agricultural shows and other rural gatherings in (for example) the UK and Australia. The rules of such contests vary according to venue and to local health, safety and animal welfare precautions. The "grease" used is most commonly vegetable oil. The winner of such a contest may receive the pig itself as the prize.

SWINE-SONG

'Never try to teach a pig to sing.
It wastes your time – and it annoys the pig.'
ROBERT HEINLEIN (1907–1988), *US science-fiction writer,*
adapting an earlier quote by WILL ROGERS, *US actor and comedian*

WHAT ARE SAUSAGE SKINS MADE OF?

Many, if not most, sausages contain some pork content. But what are the skins made of? Sausage skins – known technically as casings – are made either from natural organic material or from synthetic substitutes. Natural ones for pork sausages may be made from a layer of pig intestine that consists of collagen and from which the tough inner lining of the intestine has been removed. More commonly, however, they are made from collagen collected and processed from the pig hide to form a glutinous mass. This can then be extruded through a die to become either empty skins that can later be filled with sausage meat or a sort of thin dough that can be applied to the outside of the shaped sausage meat and hardened into a casing by treating it in an acid bath. Synthetic casings are mostly made from cellulose derived from cotton wool (unrefined absorbent cotton fibres also called linters), processed into a paste and extruded through a die. They are transparent, rather tougher than natural collagen casings, and are used particularly in the production of frankfurters (wieners) and similar types of sausage, and of course vegetarian sausage substitutes. Some cellulose casings are combined with plastic or even wood pulp for the coverings of various salamis from which the skin has to be peeled before consumption.

SERENDIPITY

'Even a blind pig finds an acorn once in a while.'
Rural saying in Edwardian England